Reconnaissance Planes since 1945

Frank Schwede

Translated by Geoffrey Brookes

Pen & Sword
AVIATION

Originally published as *Aufklärer seit 1945*
Copyright © 2014, Motorbuch Verlag, Stuttgart

First published in Great Britain in 2018 by
Pen & Sword Aviation
an imprint of
Pen & Sword Books Ltd
47 Church Street
Barnsley
South Yorkshire
S70 2AS

Copyright © Frank Schwede 2018

ISBN 978 1 47389 133 3

Typeset in Ehrhardt by
Mac Style Ltd, Bridlington, East Yorkshire
Printed and bound in India by Replika Press Pvt. Ltd

Pen & Sword Books Ltd incorporates the imprints of Pen & Sword Archaeology, Atlas, Aviation, Battleground, Discovery, Family History, History, Maritime, Military, Naval, Politics, Railways, Select, Transport, True Crime, and Fiction, Frontline Books, Leo Cooper, Praetorian Press, Seaforth Publishing and Wharncliffe.

For a complete list of Pen & Sword titles please contact
PEN & SWORD BOOKS LIMITED
47 Church Street, Barnsley, South Yorkshire, S70 2AS, England
E-mail: enquiries@pen-and-sword.co.uk
Website: www.pen-and-sword.co.uk

Contents

Air reconnaissance from aircraft has just celebrated its centenary. Coinciding with the early beginnings of aviation, in 1914 the first biplanes were ready for series production and it was fairly certain then that they would be used in the First World War for reconnaissance. Over the last hundred years they have grown in importance. Forty years ago high-flying reconnaissance aircraft such as the Lockheed U-2 or later the SR-71 were needed to fly missions for the collection of important information about a country or a whole continent. Nowadays such data can be obtained swiftly and comfortably with satellites or the use of drones. At any time and anywhere, they are in a position to gather important knowledge about the current situation e.g. from countries in crisis situations, in real time. Fom an operational area close to an altitude of 20,000 metres, for example, Global Hawk-drones can pinpoint the source of radio messages, eavesdrop mobil telephones, intercept SMS text messages and tape-record radio and television transmissions. Similar to an electronic vacuum cleaner their sensors are able to forward the most diffuse sources of emissions in the form of electro-magnetic information over three different

radio connections to a specific ground station almost in real time for evaluation of the data with scientific precision.

Readers will discover in this book a multitude of aircraft operated by the military and secret services of the United States, Europe and self-evidently also the former Soviet Union and modern Russia, for espionage and intelligence gathering over mainland and ocean. Many of these aircraft have a so-called dual role as a reconnaissance aircraft and also a fighter or bomber. Especially after the Second World War this was not a rare occurrence. Therefore numerous reconnaissance aircraft came into being after being long-distance bombers, and now excellent for the reconnaissance role by virtue of their enormous range.

This book offers the reader a representative cross-section of aircraft used worldwide for air reconnaissance, and information on their backgrounds, technical details, indications of tactical use and of course many photographs.

Frank Schwede
Feldafing, 2014

Introduction

Following the end of the Second World War the so-called Cold War began between the West, led by the United States, and the Eastern Bloc under Soviet dictatorship. The direct rivalry between the two systems was exemplified later in the armaments race of the Super Powers, and later this had as its consequence the formation of the North Atlantic Treaty Organisation (NATO) – initially limited to a period of 20 years – on 4 April 1949. The member States were the USA, Canada, France, Belgium, Denmark, Iceland, Italy, Luxembourg, Norway, Portugal, the Netherlands and Great Britain.

In response the Soviet Union now strove for the equivalent, and under its leadership in 1955 in partnership with the countries of Eastern Europe it founded the Warsaw pact. In order to scare off the other side, the striking power of the aerial forces of each organisation respectively was massively increased so that across Europe fleets of fighters and bombers from West and East confronted each other. From then on both sides saw themselves under constant threat and looked for ever new possibilities and ways of keeping the other side under control. The NATO commanders considered that the most powerful of all solutions was a mobile reconnaissance and early warning system able to detect military moves by the other side in NATO airspace in time. One of the most senior NATO commanders given the task of making a study came to the conclusion that the available fixed radar stations could no longer guarantee an effective air defence of the continental European area. This was because the Warsaw Pact already had fast fighter aircraft able to elude radar detection by low level flight. An additional danger was that the ground-based watch on the skies, whose pre-warning time was limited to a half hour, could be blinded by electronic means. It was hoped that a mobile, aerial early warning system would detect even the smaller attack formations early enough to be engaged by radar-guided interceptor fighters. For many this was the birth of modern air reconnaissance providing surface cover, but actually it went somewhat further back – a hundred years or so.

During the approximately 22 wars in Europe in the 17th century, air reconnaissance was not possible. Not until the invention of the hot air balloon in 1783 by the Montgolfiere brothers did balloon ascent begin to play an increasingly important role and enable the military to obtain an overview of the ground situation from the air – therefore air reconnaissance.

In the Franco-Prussian War the balloon was also used to some extent as an observation post which was perhaps a decisive step for air reconnaissance. The balloons rose into the air attached to a cable for the purpose of observing the enemy lines and reporting the situation without delay to the troops on the ground. In the First World War so-called *Spähballons* (spying- or lookout balloons) were used by the Germans solely as observation balloons on the Western Front where they were known as *Feldluftschiffe* (field airships). Even today the German

The lookout-gondola of the First World War was an observation car hung from a Zeppelin airship which could be lowered through cloud for air reconnaissance purposes. (Lokilech)

In the First World War so-called Spähballons *(spying- or lookout balloons) were used by the Germans solely as observation balloons on the Western Front where they were known as* Feldluftschiffe *(field airships). (Hirschfeld/ Herrmann)und Feldluftschiffer genannt. (Hirschfeld/Herrmann)*

Bundswehr uses tethered balloons fitted with cameras.

Later, during the conquest of Liege on 7 August 1914 a Zeppelin airship was involved, while at about the same time France and Great Britain used aircraft for air reconnaissance for the first time. An anonymous German pilot described a reconnaissance flight in an article published in the journal *Die Woche* on 26 September 1914 as follows:

"My flying detachment consists of several aircraft and is part of (.....) Armeekorps. We also fly reconnaissance for this Armeekorps. At the beginning there was not much confidence in aerial reconnaissance, but soon they knew better. The airfield lies some kilometres behind the command post, close to Command HQ. Here on the airfield one receives the mission. One then propellors up to about 1200 metres above the enemy. Lower is not advisable because the French rounds have got a fairly long range. I have a few holes in the wings of my aircraft to prove it. If the weather is reasonably clear, from this height one can observe quite well. Our biplanes

are very fast (about 110 km/hr) and so one can cover quite a long stretch in a short time. The observer then sketches what he has seen, and we fly back. The report is then taken by car from the airfield to Command HQ."

Thus a report by a reconnaissance pilot from 100 years ago. Nowadays, thanks to electronic imagery, pictures from the current operational area can be transmitted to the ground station in real time. It is possible today from orbit, with the aid of camera devices having an extremely high focal length, to take photographs with a resolution of less than 30 cm from 250 km distance. During the Cold War such espionage was the everyday business of the secret services and military of the Great Powers. Even today the old rule holds sway: whoever knows his enemy's next step is superior to him.

As a rule the surveillance of large areas of land is carried out from the largest reconnaissance platforms able to gather as much information as possible overflying the region just once. Accordingly in the past for this kind of operation the major Powers tended to use high-flying very fast aircraft such as the high-altitude Lockheed reconnaissance aircraft SR-71 towards the end of the 1960s which could operate from around 25 km at Mach 3. Great altitude has not only the advantage of minimal optical distortion at the picture edges, but also offers the best protection against enemy radar and enemy anti-aircraft rockets.

Surveillance and monitoring is nowadays a sensitive subject, and the Super Powers such as the United States, Russia and the remnants of the Communist bloc are no longer the only target of surveillance. The public is monitored at all places where people gather in numbers: at railway stations, airports, in pedestrian areas, in shops. Nearly every citizen has been watched somewhere. The surveillance business has therefore long been an everyday affair, even in private households, where the small spyglass in the front door is as commonplace as the letterbox. The reason is simple: security has the greatest priority, for whoever feels secure, feels good in his surroundings. Therefore many people speak of monitoring hysteria, especially data protectors do this and see the world and society as being exposed to surveillance madness.

Surveillance on the large scale, for strategic planning to secret service information, occurs today with the help of spy satellites. These watch out for troop movements or the setting up of new rocket batteries – also for significant economic changes,

especially in Communist-type countries, which in the long run also counts as important information. The border between tactical and strategic reconnaissance is as a rule fluid. In general, tactical reconnaissance is carried out at the behest of ground commanders using high performance aircraft or drones, but strategic systems can find a use for tactical reconnaissance. In very rare cases tactical reconnaissance can include surveillance. So-called strategic reconnaissance platforms must be in a position to gather as much information as possible from the greatest possible area in a single overflight of territory. For this reason in the past very high-altitude aircraft such as the legendary Lockheed U-2 were used for reconnaissance duties. Very soon, however, the USAF and CIA became painfully aware that these wonder-weapons of technology do have their weak points and are not invulnerable. Modern, high flying interceptor rockets from the opposing camp quickly made easy meat of U-2 reconnaissance aircraft so that from the beginning of the 1980s they were replaced by satellites or unmanned drones.

Modern reconnaissance proceeds with the aid of the most up-to-date technology, from the conventional digital camera to data and radio antennae, from micro-wave receivers to thermal imaging cameras and radar, and so on. It can be sub-divided into six large areas:

The high altitude reconnaissance aircraft Lockheed SR-71 can operate at a height close to 25 kilometres. (NASA)

Modern high-altitude interceptor rockets from the opposing camp made easy meat of the U-2 reconnaissance aircraft. (Reynolds/USAF)

SIGINT (SIGnal INTelligence): Conventional radio- and electronic eavesdropping, representing a constantly growing area of reconnaissance basically involving the collection of information across the entire electro-magnetic spectrum.

ELINT (ELectronic INTelligence): Pure electronic reconnaissance. ELINT is a specialized and very important form of SIGINT. All ELINT-aircraft are equipped with highly-sensitive receivers able to evaluate the electro-magnetic beams of enemy anti-radar sets. The data and information obtained can be used to put together effective counter-measures. This kind of reconnaissance is usually carried out at great altitude.

COMINT (COMunication INTelligence): Numerous countries have special COMINT aircraft able to record information from all radio frequencies. Since most of the material will be encrypted, as a rule the aircraft will carry teams of cryptanalysts for decoding purposes.

TELINT (TELemetric INTelligence): So-called telemetry reconnaissance. This is used to record all data passing between a missile, e.g. a drone or long-range rocket, and the ground control station during a test run, and is a means to obtain precise details as to the performance of a particular flying machine.

AWACS (Airborne Warning And Control System): A flying radar system. The purpose is airspace reconnaissance and surveillance from an aircraft for early recognition and warning of a threat. NATO and many other States and Great Powers have had this kind of system for over 30 years.

Depending on the spectrum of the task, a variety of aircraft types are used for reconnaissance and surveillance. For pinpointed targets small aircraft types are suitable, while for the reconnaissance of large surface areas, without the risk of exposure to air defences, large high-flying aircraft are used. Nevertheless the risks with reconnaissance flights are high even in peacetime. Up to the present around 150 USAF men have gone missing while so engaged. One of the most spectacular cases was the downing of a U-2 reconnaissance aircraft over the former Soviet Union on 1 May 1960 and the capture of its pilot Gary Powers. Another headline-maker was the shooting down of an ECE-121 by a North Korean fighter over the Sea of Japan on 15 April 1969 in which 31 crew members lost their lives. Reconnaissance flights of yesterday and today are never totally devoid of risk. Perhaps that is one of the reasons why many of today's military men are sold on unmanned drones or prefer to obtain all their information via satellites, yet for the forseeable future manned reconnaissance aircraft will still be needed.

Finally at the present time the next generation of highly modern spy-planes is being planned by the big manufacturers, for obviously even here the business of security is booming. Reconnaissance flights are for the crewman often a search for a needle in a haystack. Whether over land or the expanses of the sea.

During his research, the author had the opportunity to fly as a guest aboard a Lockheed P-2 Orion maritime reconnaissance and ASW aircraft of the German Federal Navy: his report follows.

The Orion Patrol: A Baltic Exercise
Pirates have captured a freighter off the Horn of Africa. Pirates in the 20th century? Yes, piracy is nowadays a reality and sombody well versed in it is 35-year old Kapitänleutnant (=senior lieutenant) M. Nils. He has a passion for flying and for three years has been a crewman aboard the Lockheed

P-3C Orion long-range maritime reconnaissance and ASW aircraft which the German Federal Navy has been using operationally for some years. He and his co-fliers have often been in Djibouti, the port where the Red Sea and the Gulf of Aden meet, and he knows the invisible dangers. It might be a motor boat with fishermen on board in the shallow waters off the coast, or perhaps a speedboat approaching a freighter at high speed. At the Horn of Africa, piracy is an everyday occurrence. For the people who live there, for international shipping companies, merchant shipping and for the crew of the maritime reconnaissance aircraft of the German Federal Navy. Eight hours and more per day the Orion crew spend in the air in order to lay potential pirates by the heels. The sea area around the Horn of Africa is indicated as a danger zone on nautical charts. Repeatedly in the past merchant ships have had very unpleasant meetings with the piratical fraternity, but the owners of international shipping companies accept the risk because it is on an

Reaching for the stars: a view from the cockpit of an SR-71 at around 25 kms altitude. SR-71 in knapp 25.000 m Höhe. (USAF)

international trade route. The crew of the Orion is there to protect them. Real experience on actual operations is their training school.

Change of location: Nordholz. A small village near Cuxhaven. A Tuesday morning in 2010: I am to observe a naval-air exercise simulating a situation such as occurs in the Horn of Africa. The report on the computer screen is short and to the point, and makes the seriousness of the situation clear. It is believed that pirates have seized a merchant ship. They have taken the ship's master and two seamen hostage. One seaman has been shot, the report goes on, and he needs urgent medical attention. More information is added: the situation aboard the freighter seems to be getting out of control. Everybody is nervous. The crew, the pirates and the helpers who cannot help: nobody knows exactly where the ship and its hostages are. It is clear immediately that swift action is needed in order to avoid more bloodshed. Voices are heard coming from the loudspeakers in the operations centre. They are from the crew of one of the two Tornados which has overflown the area several times. Also present are three frigates. For further support the attendance of the Lockheed P-3C Orion long-range maritime reconnaissance/ASW aircraft is required.

0800 hrs: Situation conference in the command centre of Marineflieger-Geschwader 3 *Graf Zeppelin*. The building has the shape of a box set into the landscape. It is a bunker, a safe place therefore for a time of serious crisis and for secret sessions such as this one. It is here that all threads meet this morning. Logistical precision work is routine here and lightens the load. An official pins a naval chart to the wall, on it the operational area is marked within red lines: it is assumed that the ship with the hostages aboard will

Radar signals, for the layman unintelligible strokes and threads on the screen, being matched by the surface-waters operator. (Schwede)

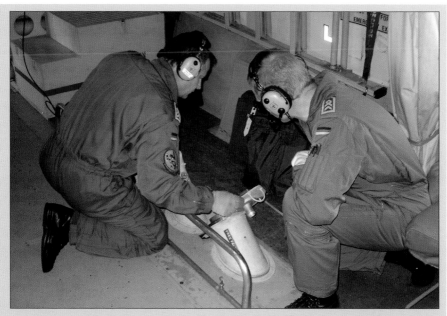

The cover of one of the total of four internal release-shafts opened to drop a sonar buoy. (Schwede)

be found within it. The Orion crew makes notes. The latest data is included, the latest details quickly discussed. There is no more time to waste, the operation must begin.

The crew is taken by staff bus to the hangar where the Lockheed Orion is parked, tanked up with 20,000 litres of kerosene. The eleven-man crew (pilot, co-pilot, flight engineer, flight electronic engineer, tactical coordinator, navigator, three sea-surface and two undersea operators) make the final preparations around and in the aircraft. The sky over Nordholz is grey and overcast, the air temperature is 10°C with a light westerly breeze. The sensors are started up, readings checked. The average time the P-3 can stay in the air without refuelling is over ten hours. This is the rule on operations overseas. This machine here with the identification mark 60+08 returned just a few weeks ago from an operation over the Horn of Africa in the framework of Operations *Enduring Freedom* and *Atalanta*. The task of the crew then as now was to secure the seaways and identify possible

pirates, to provide for vessels at sea a comprehensive picture of the situation which, for example, in operations to liberate people is not only important for the security of the forces at the location, but also for the survival of the civilian ship's crews. What begins like an adventure is in reality gruelling work which in an extreme case can very dangerous if heavy weapons come into play.

The four Allison T56-A-14 engines have meanwhile been started up and are running warm. The aircraft moves away and rolls to the airstrip. Here a Government Airbus is waiting for permission to take off – after three minutes the Orion has the green light and rolls faster and faster down the concrete flight path before winging up into the morning sky. It ascends smoothly, and after a few minutes the sea is far below. The soft waves become a uniform pattern, and then the North Sea and coast disappear beaneath a grey veil.

After an hour in the air we reach our operational zone. Work at the computer and radar stations is at full pressure. Radar signals, which for us laymen appear on the screen as indefinable streaks and threads, are evaluated. And suddenly – there is the first. White patches, which seem to combine with each other, are seen on the radar screen. False alarm! The operator had already evaluated the signal some time previously and announces that these are the islands of Fyn and Seeland off the coast of Denmark.

The search continues. Altitude 2000 feet: the four turboprops drone. Another signal appears. The data is matched, then disappointment again. A harmless fishing boat. At the rear preparations are being made to launch two sonobuoys. These are intended for thermal-, noise- and water-density measurements. A couple of turns of the hand and a hinged lid covering the four internal launch shafts opens and the first

buoy is fired. A second one follows. At the same time yellow, green and red flares appear suddenly some 20 sea miles south of Bornholm. "Red is the enemy," the operator explains, "Yellow and green are friendly frigates." That means for us that the ship with hostages has been found. Now the frigates and two Tornados take over. Our mission is completed, the exercise terminated. Obviously the reality would look rather different, the operator declares. We lose altitude to 1,000 feet. For safety reasons we don lifevests. Below us the Baltic looks a pale blue, the shadow of the Orion follows us on the surface of the sea. Giant container ships and trim yachts show up like miniatures. One moment for a touch of romance and then we head back to base.

A German Navy Lockheed PC-3 parked after being topped up with 20,000 litres of kerosene. (German Navy)

Boeing EC-135

At the beginning of the 1960s, the US Air Force began converting some of its Type KC-135 Stratotankers experimentally into airborne command posts and flying relay stations, and these were used operationally by Strategic Air Command (SAC) between 1961 and 2003. The idea was that should a complete destruction of all communications installations and command centres occur on the ground, all bombers and cruise missiles would remain operational, and that cruise missiles kept at constant readiness for defence purposes could also be fired from an EC-135. The planning also envisaged that in a crisis situation, the US President, Vice-President and Defence Minister would occupy the EC-135 as a so-called flying command post and, with the help of anti-monitoring technology, continue to exchange information with other command centres. The entire technology for this purpose was housed on the main deck, and all engines received a refuelling installation so that in an

Aircraft Type:	Boeing EC-135
Crew:	4 flight deck personnel + 19 operators
Engine:	4 x Pratt & Whitney TF33-PW-102 (8000 kg thust)
Wingspan:	39.9 m
Length:	43.1 m
Height:	12.7 m
Wing surface:	226 m²
Top speed:	910 km/hr
Cruising speed:	800 km/hr
Max. rate of climb:	1,490 m/min
Service ceiling:	13,400 m
Range:	4,300 km

emergency the operational endurance of the aircraft in flight could be extended indefinitely.

These operational flights with the EC-135 were given the codename "Looking Glass" and started up

The plans envisaged that in a crisis situation, the US President, Vice-President and Defence Minister would use an EC-135 as a so-called flying command post. (Lopez/USAF)

The complement consisted of the flight crew (pilot, co-pilot, navigator and engineer), and ten to fourteen other crew. (USAF)

in February 1961. By the end of 1962 the fleet of machines used for the purpose had grown to 16, at the height of the Cold War the SAC had around 71 machines available from time to time.

The Looking Glass missions tours of duty lasted eight hours as a rule but could be lengthened if the need arose. The complement consisted of the flight crew (pilot, co-pilot, navigator and engineer), and ten to fourteen other crew including the SAC commander, operations leader, signals specialists, experts in data interpretation, meteorologist and several radio technicians. The machines operated from various bases across the United States. From 3 February 1964 until 24 July 1990 there was always one machine of the Looking Glass mission airborne. The flights per day were then reduced to one until the SAC was disbanded on 1 June 1992, and from 1993 the entire EC-135 fleet was grounded for reasons of economy and because improved satellite technology had become available.

Later, NASA took eight EC-135s from the USAF to support its Apollo missions. These aircraft received the designation EC-135N ARIA (Apollo Range Instrumentation Aircraft) and were each given a US$4 million conversion including a 3-metre long radar dome, the so-called Snoopy Nose, with steerable parabolic tracking antennae to relay radio conversations and telemetric data: transmitter and receiver for contact with space vehicles and the ground station at Houston, data processing equipment, magnetic tape recorders and cine cameras. The ARIA fleet was stationed at the Patrick air force base in Florida, and its first operation in April 1968 supported the Apollo-6 mission. The aim was to constantly maintain the best possible radio contact between the spacecraft and Houston: the ARIA's were also responsible for establishing the initial radio contact between Houston and the Apollo crew after re-entry into the Earth's atmosphere.

From 3 February 1964 until 24 July 1990 there was always one EC-135 machine of the "Looking Glass Mission" airborne. From 1993 the entire fleet was grounded for budgetary reasons. (Jose Lopez/USAF)

Following the closing down of the Apollo programme, the ARIA machines accompanied numerous civilian and military rocket and satellite projects. The last EC-135 ARIA aircraft was decommissioned in November 2000 and is now exhibited at the USAF Museum in Ohio.

Snoopy-Nose: NASA took eight EC-135s from the USAF to support its Apollo missions. These aircraft received the designation EC-135N ARIA. (Greg Hume)

Boeing P-8 *Poseidon*

Development work on the Boeing P-8 was begun in the mid-1980s. In collaboration with the US Navy, the US Government was looking for a suitable and above all powerful successor for the already ageing Lockheed P-3 Orion. Because of budgetary shortages, the primary objective for the new aircraft was to operate at lower cost. This would be brought about by the use of more stable materials: in comparison the Navy pointed to the comparative high rate of materials fatigue of the P-3 which in the course of a year drove maintenance costs sky-high. Furthermore the Pentagon wanted the new model to have a substantially greater range combined with a reduction in the overall weight. The 1989 development contract was awarded initially to Lockheed, but their design for the successor P-7 never entered production, the contract being rescinded a year later for exceeding the expenditure limit by US$300 million. Once the Cold War ended, the US Government saw no further need for the project which was therefore put on ice and the entire Orion fleet given a more cost-favourable modernization programme.

In the year 2000 the US Government decided upon a new development programme for which only Lockheed-Martin and Boeing would compete. Lockheed submitted a turbo-prop variant in a model designated Orion 21. Boeing on the other hand was already planning a modified version of its proven passenger aircraft 737-800ERX. A year later the British manufacturer BAE-Systems tendered a proposal for the BAE Nimrod MRA4, already developed for the RAF, but in October 2002 the British tender was withdrawn after it was recognized that for political reasons it hardly stood any chance challenging the powerful US competition.

On 14 June 2004 the US$3.9 million MMA programme was decided in Boeing's favour, and on 8

Aircraft Type:	Boeing P-8 Poseidon
Purpose:	Maritime reconnaissance and ASW aircraft
Crew:	2 pilots + 7 operators
Engine:	4 x CFM International CFM56-7B each of 12,000 kgs thrust
Wingspan:	37.64 m
Length:	39.47m
Height:	12.83m
Wing surface:	n/a
Top speed:	906 km/hr
Cruising speed:	789 km/hr
Max. rate of climb:	n/a
Service ceiling:	12,500 m
Range:	2,200 km (4 hours stay in target area)
Reichweite	2.200 km (4 Stunden Aufenthalt im Zielgebiet)

Boeing P-8 Poseidon: a modified version of the proven passenger aircraft 737-800ERX. (Lucht USN)

July that year the US Navy gave them the green light for the production of the first five machines.

On 25 April 2009 the P-8A absolved its maiden flight, and in October 2010 the first sonobuoy-launch tests were carried out. For the coming years the US Government is planning to buy 117 of these aircraft using them as gradual replacements for the P-3 Orion.

Meanwhile India has also become a user of the P-8, and in 2009 ordered from Boeing eight P-8I valued at US$2 billion. The machines are based on the P-8A developed for the US Navy although Indian manufacturers were involved in equipping the aircraft. The P-8I is armed inter alia with Harpoon guided weapons, Mk 54 torpedoes and Mk 82 depth charges. Delivery began in 2013 and was expected to be completed in 2015. Canada and Australia have also reported their interest but in 2008 Italy withdrew its acquisition plans.

For the coming years the US Government is planning to buy 117 of these aircraft using them as gradual replacements for the P-3 Orion. (Lovelady USN)

Boeing RC-135

The history of the Boeing RC-135 goes back to the beginning of the 1960s when the USAF was looking for a military reconnaissance aircraft to engender a new generation. Formerly old bombers had been converted into reconnaissance aircraft for this purpose, but the electronic age of aerial reconnaissance had dawned and now the time was ripe for a new and above all suitable new generation of aircraft. During their search, high ranking representatives of the Strategic Air Command (SAC), of the USAF and Defence Ministry noticed the medium and long-range transport aircraft Boeing C-135 Stratolifter.

On board the converted aircraft is special equipment for strategic electronic reconnaissance (ELINT) and communications monitoring (COMINT),

Aircraft Type:	Boeing RC-135
Purpose:	Strategic reconnaissance
Crew:	5 flight deck crew + 22 operators
Engine:	4 x CFM International F108-CF-201 (each 8900 kgs thrust)
Wingspan:	39.90 m
Height:	12.8 m
Wing surface:	226 m²
Top speed:	900 km/hr
Cruising speed:	n/a
Max. rate of climb:	1,490 m/min
Service ceiling:	13,400 m
Range:	6,500 km

In 2007 there were still 22 RC-135s of the S,U,V and W versions in service with the USAF. (USAF)

On board the converted aircraft is special equipment for strategic electronic reconnaissance (ELINT) and communications monitoring (COMINT). (Nolan/USAF)

recognizable outwardly by the enlarged radar dome at the nose for the expanded radar technology and the "fat cheeks" for the aerodynamic disguising of the sensors on both sides of the fuselage.

Over the course of time more than ten different variants of the original RC-135 emerged of which deserving special mention is the RC-135S Cobra Ball, the main purpose of which during the Cold War was to observe Soviet intercontinental rockets tests and which from 1964 was stationed by SAC at the Eilson AF base in Alaska. Flights were made as a rule in contact with land- and sea-based radar installations in Alaska. After the end of the Cold War the operational flights of the Cobra Ball were substantially reduced. Not until after the outbreak of the Guilf War at the beginning of the 1990s did the tally of operational flights increase – this time over Iraq and neighbouring States. The purpose of these missions

was to obtain a precise idea of how the Iraqis operated their medium-range rockets.

The RC-135S crew usually consists of four cockpit crew and twelve specialists and technicians. In 2007 there were still 22 RC-135s of the S,U,V and W versions in service with the USAF. The machines are deployed by 55.Strategic Reconnaissance Squadron attached to Air Combat Command with its seat at the Offut AF base in Nebraska. Versions V and W are designated "Rivet Joint" and from their technical equipment are basically the successor model to the RC-135. During the Cold War they were deployed along the Soviet border amongst other places under the codename "Burning Wind". Their missions supplied important information about troop movements and relocations in the Eastern Bloc States, and they also operated in the pursuit of the Achille Lauro hi-jackers in 1985 and in the US "Just

The RC-135S "Cobra Ball" on the way to its operational area. At the time of the Cold War its main purpose was to observe Soviet intercontinental rocket tests. The Cobra Ball fleet was stationed by SAC at the Eilson AF base in Alaska. (USAF)

Cause" invasion of Panama in 1989. Since the outbreak of the Gulf War in the 1990s States of the Near East have used these reconnaissance aircraft increasingly. On board the Rivet Joints up to 27 specialists work on all kinds of electronic and radio signals reconnaissance.

In future besides the USAF the British RAF will also have the RC-135 as a replacement for their already obsolete Nimrod fleet. The Labour Government under Gordon Brown decided to procure three machines of this series to be given the internal designation Airseeker. The training of the future crews was started in January 2011 and the three aircraft are expected to be delivered in 2017.

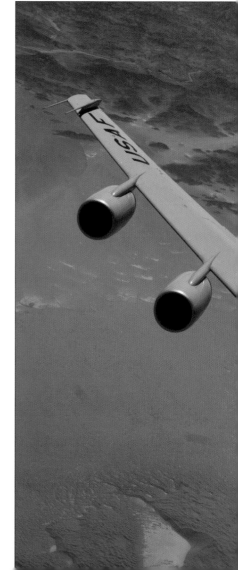

OPP Fat cheeks" for the aerodynamic covering over of the sensors on both sides of the fuselage. (Cheung/USAF)

On board the RC-135 is special equipment for strategic electronic reconnaissance (ELINT) and communications monitoring (COMINT), recognizable outwardly by the enlarged radar dome at the nose for the expanded radar technology. (Alan Brown)

Boeing E-3A *Sentry*

In 1965 the US Defence Ministry began work on an airborne warning and control system, AWACS for short, and co-opted Boeing as a partner. The result of seven-years development work was the Boeing E-3A Sentry. Its striking feature is the huge discus-shaped rotating biped dome of 9.1 metres diameter containing the main radar antenna. From an altitude of around 9,150 metres the radar is able to encompass 312,000 km² of the Earth's surface, the area monitored extending from the ground to the stratosphere. Even the movement of enemy shipping can be pinpointed within a range of 400 kms. The radar fills a large section of the fuselage rear immediately behind the wings although the core of the installation is beneath the rotodome where the echo of the radar beams is received. A choice had to be made between the Air Force radars of the firms Westinghouse and Hughes: after 625 hours of testing the USAF decided in favour of the Westinghouse APY-1 Impulse-Doppler high-frequency pursuit radar for measuring range and

Aircraft Type:	Boeing E-3 Sentry
Purpose:	Reconnaissance aircraft
Crew:	**E3-A:** 17 (4 flight deck crew + 13 operators) **E3-B&C:** 21 (4 flight deck crew + 17 operators)
Engine:	4 x CFM 56-2 turbofans with 10,676 kgs thrust (aircraft sold to foreign military) or 4 x CFM turbofans TF33 PW-100 A with 9,341 kgs thrust (US/NATO aircraft)
Wingspan:	44.43 m
Length:	46.62 m
Height:	12.70 m
Wing surface:	283 m²
Top speed:	858 km/hr
Cruising speed:	c. 800 km/hr
Max. rate of climb:	8.7 m/sec
Service ceiling:	c. 12,500 m
Range:	over 9,250 km

Some of the NATO Boeing AWACS fleet require special approval to fly because the E-3A engines no longer comply with today's strict environmental regulations. (NATO)

The history of the Sentry began towards the end of the 1960s when Boeing received from the US Defence Ministry a contract to build two prototype long-range AWACS reconnaissance aircraft. (Boeing)

The crew of the Mission Deck is responsible for assessing the aerial situation and providing tactical support to fighters and fighter-bombers by radio and data link. (Kelling/USN)

The striking feature of the Sentry is the huge discus-shaped rotating biped dome containing the main radar antenna situated on the fuselage between the wings and tailplane. (USAF)

speed based on the evaluation of radar impulses reflected from various targets.

The history of the Sentry began towards the end of the 1960s when Boeing received from the US Defence Ministry a contract to build two prototype long-range AWACS reconnaissance aircraft. At first a completely new design was planned but then abandoned on grounds of cost, Boeing and the Ministry opting instead for the well-proven four-engined Boeing 707. The first AWACS protoype EC-137D (the USAF internal designation for this model) had its maiden flight on 9 February 1972 but the first machines of a total of 34 AWACS aircraft built did not enter USAF service until 1977. NATO stationed the first of 17 Boeing E-3A at the NATO Geilenkirchen base on 24 February 1982. The number of crew aboard these aircraft is generally seventeen, divided between the so-called Flight Deck and Mission Deck. The Flight Deck crew flies the machine to the operational area where the Mission Deck contingent is responsible for assessing the aerial situation and providing tactical support to fighters and fighter-bombers by radio and data link.

Some of the NATO Boeing AWACS fleet require special approval to fly because the E-3A engines no longer comply with today's strict environmental regulations regarding exhaust gases and noise. Only the British E-3D and the French E-3F are fitted with more modern engines. The re-engining of the NATO E-3A types failed to go ahead when various nations involved declined to meet the capital expenditure. A total of 68 aircraft of this type left the Boeing work halls.

The first machines of a total of 34 AWACS aircraft built entered USAF service in 1977. (McDowell)

NATO stationed the first of 17 Boeing E-3A at the NATO Geilenkirchen base on 24 February 1982. (NATO)

Boeing E-6 *Mercury*

The Boeing E-6 Mercury, also known as E-6 TACAMO (Take Charge and Move Out) has its roots in the Cold War when contact with nuclear-armed submarines on the world's oceans was essential. From the mid-1960s the US Navy used for this task a Lockheed C-130 Hercules specially converted for the purpose, but by the early 1980s it had reached the end of the road and the Defence Ministry now found it necessary to find a suitable successor. Because Boeing had extensive experience from their E-3 Sentry model, it was logical that on 29 April 1983 the concern should be awarded the contract to develop the E-6A on the basis of the Boeing 707-320B. The maiden flight took place on 19 February 1987 but numerous technical problems delayed the entry of the machines into service until 2 August 1989, at Barber's Point, Hawaii. Boeing completed 16 more aircraft of this type between 1989 and 1992.

From 1985, twelve aircraft designated E-6 Mercury II were fitted with additional special communications technology to be used for direct contact with land-based ICBM's in a crisis situation. From 1 October that year the E-6 fleet also took over the Looking Glass Mission flights from the decommissioned EC-135Cs. For this purpose it was

Aircraft Type:	Boeing E-6 Mercury
Purpose:	Command aircraft
Crew:	22
Engine:	4 x CFM International CFM56-2A-2
Wingspan:	45.16 m
Length:	46.61 m
Height:	12.93 m
Wing surface:	283.4 m²
Top speed:	981 km/hr
Cruising speed:	842 km/hr
Max. rate of climb:	n/a
Service ceiling:	12,800 m
Range:	11,700 km

necessary to transfer the comprehensive electronic equipment from the EC-135s into the E-6s. Accordingly all E-6A's had been refitted as E-6B's by the end of 2003 and carried the characteristic radar bulge containing all the MILSTAR electronics with aerials on the fuselage roof at the level of the wing roots. It is planned to maintain the E-6 in service until 2030 at the latest.

The Boeing E-6 Mercury has its roots in the Cold War when it was essential to maintain contact at all times with nuclear-armed submarines on the world's oceans. (USN)

The maiden flight of the E-6 Mercury took place on 19 February 1987 but numerous technical problems delayed the entry of the machines into service until 2 August 1989, at Barber's Point, Hawaii.

Between 1989 and 1992 Boeing completed 16 more aircraft of this type. (Radecki)

The characteristic radar bulge on the fuselage roof forward contains all the MILSTAR electronics with aerials. It is planned to maintain the E-6B in service until 2030 at the latest. (Bidini)

Canadair CL-28 *Argus*

In 1954 the Canadian aircraft manufacturer Canadair began work on its CL-28 to replace the ageing Avro Lancaster A10 and Lockheed P2V Neptune currently serving with RCAF Maritime Air Command. The CL-28 was incidentally the largest aircraft built in Canada and based on the Bristol Britannia so that the wings, tailplane and undercarriage of both models were identical. It was necessary to restructure and reinforce the fuselage to take two weapons bays, and a pressurized cabin was dispensed with on account of the low operational ceiling.

The first protoype Argus 1 had its maiden flight on 28 March 1957; two further machines of the Mk 1 standard with a US APS-20 radar in a radome below the cockpit followed. 20 later examples of the Argus had a British radar in a smaller radome.

The Argus usually flew with a 15-man crew: three pilots, two flight engineers, three navigators and seven ASW operators. During a patrol the crew worked up to 20 hours and more with a shift system. A galley and cots were fitted at the rear of the machine. The most important crew positions were the glazed nose for the observer, the flight deck for the pilot, co-pilot and flight engineers, behind them the places for the navigator and radio operator. The members of the seven-strong ASW team were at the rear under the direction of the tactical coordinator with two observation seats behind them. The ASW equipment of the CL-28 included a search radar, a magnetic anomaly detector, defensive electronics and a diesel-fume detector. Sonobuoys, starshell and sea markers were housed in a store at the rear. The weapons of attack consisted of acoustic torpedoes and depth charges located in the two interior weapons bays. The Argus could also serve as a minelayer or transporter. Production of the CL-28 was terminated in July 1960 with the last of 33 completed machines for the RCAF, and in 1972 permission to fly the Argus was withdrawn because of massive problems involving the undercarriage.

Aircraft Type:	Canadair CL-28 Argus
Purpose:	Maritime reconnaissance and ASW aircraft
Crew:	15
Engine:	4 x Wright R-3350 TC18EA1 Turbo-compound motors (4 x 2,535 kW)
Wingspan:	43.37 m
Length:	39.26 m
Height:	11.79 m
Wing surface:	192.77 m^2
Top speed:	507 km/hr
Cruising speed:	333 km/hr
Max. rate of climb:	n/a
Service ceiling:	7,620 m
Range:	9,495 km

In the mid-1950s the CL-28 was the largest aircraft built in Canada and based on the Bristol Britannia. (Canadair)

Lockheed U-2 *Dragon Lady*

On 4 August 1955 the first high-altitude reconnaissance aircraft of the USAF, the Lockheed U-2, took off on its maiden flight from the Edwards air force base under conditions of the strictest security. Equipped with panoramic and visual infra-red cameras and radar, the single-engined U-2 operated for more than two decades at over 20 kilometres altitude and was therefore for some time beyond the range of the ground air defences and fighters of the Communist Eastern bloc. This enormous performance was due to its design derived in some respects from the glider. Because of the enormous altitude the pilot was seated in a pressurized cockpit and wore an astronaut-type

Aircraft Type:	Lockheed U-2A
Purpose:	High altitude reconnaissance aircraft
Crew:	1
Engine:	1 x Pratt & Whitney J57-P-37A turbojet
Wingspan:	24.34 m
Length:	15.24 m
Height:	4.57 m
Wing surface:	52.5 m²
Top speed:	794 km/hr
Cruising speed:	n/a
Max. rate of climb:	n/a
Service ceiling:	21,335 m
Range:	4,800 km

Equipped with panoramic and visual infra-red cameras and radar, the single-engined U-2 operated for more than two decades as an important reconnaissance instrument for the United States. Its typical operational altitude was at more than 20 kilometres. (Reynolds/USAF)

Because of the enormous altitude the pilot was seated in a pressurized cockpit and wore an astronaut-type pressure suit. (USAF) decades as an important reconnaissance instrument for the United States. Its typical operational altitude was at more than 20 kilometres. (Reynolds/USAF)

pressure suit for protection against a sudden drop in cabin pressure or an emergency evacuation of the aircraft.

Development work on the Lockheed U-2 was begun at the manufacturer's Advanced Development Projects Unit in the early 1950s. At the suggestion of the then CIA-Director Allen Dulles, whose organisation deployed the aircraft later, the US Government awarded Lockheed a US$22.5 million contract to produce the first 20 machines. Towards the end of the 1960s Lockheed offered a larger variant designated U-2R with a wingspan of 31.7 metres, which flew for the first time on 28 August 1967, and a two-seater TR-1B, later U-2S.

Operating for a substantial time undiscovered, the aircraft U-2 Dragon Lady became probably the world's most famous spy-plane five years after its official inaugural flight. On 1 May 1960 a U-2 flown by Francis Gary Powers over the Urals was discovered by Soviet ground defences and shot

down by an S-75 anti-aircraft rocket. The aircraft entered an uncontrollable spin and Powers had to eject. The Soviets put him on trial and he was given a long prison sentence. For the US-Government this was a humiliation which was to have far-reaching consequences for the crews of the aircraft. In future the U-2s would not be equipped with an ejector seat. The reason given to the Press was short and terse: Espionage is a dangerous game and the crew of a damaged reconnaissance aircraft who fall into enemy hands can quickly become a national security risk.

At the beginning of the 1960s satellite reconnaissance began to replace U-2 operations increasingly, but the aircraft continued to succumb to tragic situations, either shot down by enemy rockets or lost as the result of technical malfunction at take-off or landing.

Up until the official halt to production in1989, 27 aircraft of this type had left the Lockheed assembly

Reunion of spies: The high-altitude reconnaissance aircraft Lockheed U-2 side by side with an AWACS Boeing E-3 Sentry. (Scott/Sturkol/USAF)

A rare guest on the aircraft carrier USS America: the high-altitude reconnaissance aircraft Lockheed U-2 after landing. (US Navy)

Nikita Khrushchev looking over the remnants of the shot-down Lockheed U-2. (CIA)

NASA used the U-2 as a civilian research aircraft with equipment for satellite communication on top of the fuselage. (Landis/NASA)

lines. Besides the USAF and CIA, NASA also used the U-2 as a civilian research aircraft. Under the designation ER-2 (ER=Earth Resources) it was used for purposes which included research of the Earth's surface and the ozone layer, and also collected important information on acid rain or the consequences of volcanic eruptions for those regions affected. In contrast to the SR-71, the U-2 was produced in much greater numbers and is today in operational use worldwide.

Under the designation ER-2 (ER=Earth Resources) the U-2 was used for purposes which included research of the Earth's surface and the ozone layer. (NASA)

Lockheed P2V
Neptune

The first studies for a land-based patrol aircraft for the US Navy were made by the Lockheed subsidiary Vega in 1941, but on account of the pressing need for aircraft from shortly before 1939 and during the Second World War the project under prototype designation XP2V-1 was not taken up until 1944. Meanwhile the US Navy had seen the need for an aircraft of this type, and Lockheed was of the opinion that the XP2V-1 could be adapted to meet the wishes of the Navy without much difficulty. Accordingly in 1944 contracts were signed for the building of two prototypes and 14 series machines, and the first prototype made its maiden flight on 17 May 1945. Delivery to the US Navy of the over 100 machines ordered began six months later. The end of the Second World War led to a stoppage in production, and it was not until September 1946 that 30 aircraft of the meanwhile further-developed P2V-2 were ordered by the US Navy. The P2V-2 had a fuselage longer by 0.76 m, modified armament and variable pitch four-blade propellors replacing the former

Aircraft Type:	Lockheed P-2V-2 Neptune
Purpose:	ASW and maritime reconnaissance aircraft
Crew:	7
Engine:	2 x Wright R-3350-24W (2 x 2,090 kW)
Wingspan:	30.5 m
Length:	23.8 m
Height:	8.94 m
Wing surface:	92.90 m²
Top speed:	515 km/hr
Cruising speed:	287 km/hr
Max. rate of climb:	n/a
Weight empty:	22,650 kg
Service ceiling:	7.925 m
Range:	6,410 km

three-bladed propellors to suit the more powerful engines. The first machines of this series run were delivered from 1947. The maiden flight of the P2V-3 with a more powerful Wright R-3350-26W was made in August 1948.

After the end of the Second World War the US Navy recognized the urgent need for a carrier-borne

A total of 1,118 Neptunes were built in over 30 different variants and were operational with twelve countries. (Lockheed Martin)

The Neptune was used operationally in the Korean and Vietnam Wars and elsewhere, and particularly during the Cuba crisis in the reconnaissance role. (USN)

Numerous Neptunes were still to be found with reserve units towards the end of the 1970s so that the P2V became one of the longest-serving military aircraft of all time. (USN)

nuclear weapons squadrons. A contract was issued for the North American AJ Savage to fill the role, but as this aircraft type would not become available until 1949 the Navy was forced to seek an alternative. After much deliberation the Navy commanders eventually decided that the only aircraft in current service suitable for a 4,500 kg bomb payload was the Neptune. Lockheed received an order for twelve P2V-C3, and between September 1948 and 1950 the batch arrived at the specially formed Composite Heavy Attack Squadron VC-5 at Moffet Field. From January 1950 the VC-6 Squadron was made operational as a nuclear bomber fleet aboard aircraft carriers.

A total of 1,118 Neptunes were built in over 30 different variants and were operational with twelve countries. Especially in the 1950s the Neptune came to the fore as the most important US Navy submarine hunter, and also came to note as a maritime reconnaissance aircraft. The Neptune was used operationally in the Korean and Viet Nam Wars and elsewhere, and particularly during the Cuba crisis in the reconnaissance role. During its long career the aircraft underwent numerous modernization programmes: not until 1970 did the last operational squadron VP-23 decommission their remaining SP-2H. Numerous Neptunes were still to be found with reserve units towards the end of the 1970s so that the P2V became one of the longest-serving military aircraft of all time.

Lockheed P-3C *Orion*

The Lockheed P-3C Orion has been deployed successfully for over three decades in 16 countries as an ASW and maritime reconnaissance aircraft and is a military version of the commercial Lockheed L-188 Electra. Its career extends back to 1957 when the US Navy began looking for a suitable successor to the ageing ASW and maritime reconnaissance aircraft P-2 Neptune. The new machine would have more space, larger range and, of special importance for reconnaissance operations, longer endurance over the operational area. Also wanted was a short-phase development term and the most economic possible systems cost. Initially this requirement was found to be insoluble by the aircraft industry and finally recourse was had to an already existing civilian aircraft. Lockheed proposed a solution based on the L-188A Electra which had been under development since 1955. Its engines were the proven Allison T56-A-10W already in use for the C-130 Hercules and which met the requirement for fast transits to operational areas, low fuel consumption at low altitudes and safe slow-speed properties in anti-submarine warfare. Not least the fact that Lockheed was highly competent in the anti-submarine detection field resulted in their being

Aircraft Type:	Lockheed P-3 Orion
Purpose:	ASW and maritime reconnaissance aircraft
Crew:	11
Engine:	2 x Rolls-Royce Allison T56-A-14 each of 4,910 hp
Wingspan:	30.37 m
Length:	35.61 m
Height:	10.27m
Wing surface:	120.77 m²
Top speed:	761 km/hr at 4,575 m
Cruising speed:	639 km/hr
Max. rate of climb:	10 m/sec
Service ceiling:	8,625 m
Range:	7,728 km

awarded the contract for the new reconnaissance aircraft.

The project known as Lockheed Model 185 was more than just a simple variant of the Electra. For reasons of weight, the fuselage had to be shortened by 2.13 metres and the cabin completely redesigned in order to install all the technical equipment. A weapons and transport bay was integrated into the

The Lockheed P-3C Orion has been deployed successfully for over three decades in 16 countries as an ASW and maritime reconnaissance aircraft. (Bundeswehr/Marine)

The career of the Lockheed P-3 Orion extends back to 1957 when the US Navy began looking for a suitable successor to the ageing ASW and maritime reconnaissance aircraft P-2 Neptune. (USN)

leading third of the fuselage, also lengthened for the purpose, all regular windows were removed in favour of five very large portholes with convex glass for the observation stations, and even the cockpit window arrangement was modified, five large windows replacing the former seven relatively small ones. The design of the fuselage nose and tail was also changed to accommodate forward- and backward-looking radars. Finally the long dome of artificial materials typical of the submarine hunter was mounted at the rear carrying the MAD (Magnetic Anomaly Detector), which registers disturbances in the Earth's magnetic field possibly caused by a submarine.

The Orions used by the Federal German Navy were taken over by the Netherlands Air Force in 2006 after having first passed to Marineflieger-Geschwader 3 in the framework of the CUP (Capabilities Upkeep Programme) for modernization at Lockheed-Martin to improve the reconnaissance capability. This included a modern Data Management System (DMS), not only for linking up the individual work places in the aircraft but also for exchanging information via UHF- and satellite connections with other units. Also new is the AN/ALR-95 Electronic Support Measures system: the data obtained can be transmitted by means of DMS digitally or encrypted to the command centres of national or friendly forces. The AN/APS-137 B(V)5 radar has so-called Synthetic Aperture Radar (SAR) and Imaging SAR (ISAR) capabilities. For self-protection the German Orions have the radar warning receiver AN/AAR 47 and the AN/ALE 47 anti-radar lure system. Furthermore completely new computers with high-definition screens have been fitted for anti-submarine work.

In comparison to the predecessor Breguet Atlantic, which flew from Nordholz for the last time in June 2010, the PC-3 has only eleven instead of twelve crew, the navigator taking over the radio operator's role. A new task for the flight electronics technician is to oversee and guarantee the running of the avionics.

The Lockheed P-3 is used not only by the military. The US meteorological authority National Oceanic and Atmospheric Administration (NOAA) operates two P-3 versions WP-3D specially for the collection and evaluation of meteorological data: the US Department of Commerce has four WP-3D which function as meteorological aircraft and so-called Hurricane Hunters. The US Customs and Border Protection (CBP) uses six P-3AEW&C as early-warning aircraft with aerial surveillance radar used in the anti-narcotics war.

The P-3 has also made a name for itself in the USA as the most popular extinguisher-aircraft for forest fires. The Aero Union Corporation organisation from the California Chico maintains and charters the machines for the entire United States.

The US Customs and Border Protection (CBP) uses six P-3AEW&C as early-warning aircraft with aerial surveillance radar used in the anti-narcotics war. (CBP)

A US Navy Lockheed P-3B Orion on patrol above the Hawaiian islands. (US Navy)

Lockheed SR-71 Blackbird

The Lockheed SR 71 is probably the best kept secret in aviation history. Its beginnings are to be found towards the end of the 1950s in a small office at CIA headquarters Langley, a surburban area north-west of Washington. Concerns had existed there for some time at the growing threat from Soviet rockets to the extremely successful but relatively slow photo-reconnaissance aircraft U-2.

In the absence of a State contract and finance initially, the two large US aircraft manufacturers Lockheed and Convair were inspired in the autumn of 1957 to prepare plans for a suitable successor to the U-2. At the end of August 1959 the decision fell in favour of Lockheed whose project A-12 "Oxcart" was immediately given the highest security rating: Chief Designer Clarence "Kelly" Johnson took over leadership and planning of the development work on the new wonder weapon.

Aircraft Type:	Lockheed SR-71
Purpose:	High altitude reconnaissance aircraft
Crew:	1
Engine:	2 x Pratt & Whitney J58 jet with afterburner, 15,130 kg thrust
Wingspan:	16.94 m
Length:	33.74 m
Height:	5.63m
Wing surface:	149.10 m^2
Top speed:	3,529 km/hr
Cruising speed:	3,219 km/hr
Max. rate of climb:	n/a
Service ceiling:	24,385 m
Range:	4,800 km

The problems seen to confront Johnson and his staff soon exceeded all the requirements with which an aircraft manufacturer has to comply. The F-104 Starfighter, born of Kelly's genius, was already in series production, and had touched Mach 2 for a few minutes at 18,290 metres altitude, but his new design had to fly at Mach 3 at above 20,000 metres for long periods. Already by then far higher Mach-values had been attained by rocket propelled test aircraft such as the North American X-15 in the thinner air layers of the upper atmosphere, but not for long and not with conventional engines.

Together with refined aerodynamics, perhaps a slender fuselage shape or thin wings together with flattened-out fuselage sides forward to prevent the nose sinking at Mach 3, heat-resistant materials were needed particularly for the bodywork and windows which had to be able to withstand friction from high temperatures of around 500°C for long periods. Similarly high requirements applied to the engines and the overall flying system. Practically every individual part of the completed aircraft, constructed for the most part of titanium B-120 down to the smallest screw, cables and quartz glass of the camera

Top secret: Clarence "Kelly" Johnson took over leadership and planning of the A-12 project "Oxcart". (CIA)

The reconnaissance sensors of the SR-71 can monitor a surface area of 250,000 km² per flight hour flown. (NASA)

windows, had to be newly developed in the briefest space of time.

Johnson decided on two original, combined jet turbine-ramjet JT11 D alias J58 Pratt & Whitney engines, the turbine section being used only for take-off and landing. The thrust for the supersonic speeds came from the ramjet section. The newly developed special fuel PF-1/LF-2A alias JP-7 of low inflammability was decided upon for the temperature range of -67°C to +340°C. Strict criteria applied even to the choice of pilots who were to be no taller than 1.83 m (6 ft 0 ins) and weigh no more than 79 kg (12 stone 6lbs).

By reason of the programme complexity, above all the problems which suddenly came to light in the construction of the titanium wings and engines, the maiden flight of the A-12 was postponed from 31 May 1961 to the end of April 1962, but even at this

OPP: Strict criteria applied even to the choice of pilots who were to be no taller than 1.83 m (6 ft 0 ins) and weigh no more than 79 kg (12 stone 6lbs).

The world's most secret and fastest reconnaissance aircraft, the Lockheed SR-71, was built in the hangars of the Skunk Works in the 1960s. (CIA)

The first SR-71A were delivered to the USAF in 1966, but were only operational to a limited extent due to technical problems. (NASA)

point Johnson and his team still had no airworthy J58 engine available, and they had to fall back on the weaker J75. Finally on 26 April 1962, 32 months after the signing of the contracts and under the greatest secrecy, the first A-12 took off on its maiden flight from the 6-km long runway of a former salt lake within the legendary "Area 51" air base at Groom Lake, Nevada.

The first reconnaissance flight proper was not made until 31 May 1967, over North Korea. The 29th and and last flight of the A-1 terminated on 8 May 1968.

Three A-12s were converted a short time later to a modified standard model prototype for the Mach 3 interceptor fighter YF-12A whose purpose was planned as the air defence role against Soviet supersonic bombers.

The basic YF-12 took off for its maiden flight on 7 August 1963 equipped with a Hughes AGS-18 radar and infra-red search unit. Three Type Hughes AIM-47B Falcon rockets were planned as armament. Ultimately the YF-12 never flew regular missions and was later passed to NASA for supersonic research. However, one machine from the

"Kelly" Johnson had to design something which would fly at Mach 3 at above 20,000 metres for long periods. (NASA)

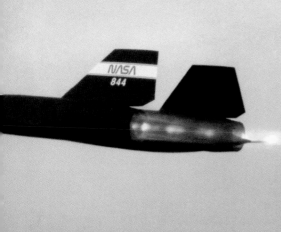

Heat-resistant building materials were needed which had to be able to withstand friction from high temperatures of around 500ºC for long periods. (NASA)

production series was later given a longer fuselage for a second cockpit window and additional fuel, and designated YF-12C. This machine became one of the SR-71 prototypes.

The first SR-71 made its maiden flight on 22 December 1964 from Palmdale, California piloted by Robery Gilliland. In January 1966 the first machine of this type entered service at 420oth Strategic Reconnaissance Wing at Beale Air Force base, California. The SR-71 was heavier than the A-12, had a longer fuselage and a 2% greater angle of attack. The first SR-71A's were delivered to the USAF in 1966 but were only operational to a limited extent due to technical problems. A B-71 bomber version designed by Kelly Johnson got no further than the planning stage. The reconnaissance sensors of the SR-71 could monitor a surface area of

250,000 km² per flight hour flown. In the years following, 32 machines of the type left the assembly lines at Skunk Works. These aircraft were exclusively double-seaters, of which 12 were lost to accidents, two were converted later to SR-71B training machines and another was modified as an SR-71C. By 1988 the number of operational machines was down to six, and in November 1989 all were decommissioned. The Blackbirds were endowed to various museums in subsequent years, three went to NASA on 15 February 1990 for research into, and development of, future civilian and military supersonic aircraft. Another customer interested in the Blackbird, for stellar observation, was the University of California.

Between 1972 and 1989 the SR-71 flew 17,300 times, of which 3,551 were reconnaissance

The first A-12 made its maiden flight on 26 April 1962. (USAF)

Johnson decided on two original, combined turbine-ramjet JT11 D alias J58 Pratt & Whitney engines. (NASA)

missions. In its more than 25-year career the SR-71 set a considerable number of records. In September 1974 a Blackbird made a transatlantic flight from New York to Farnborough in southern England in one hour, 55 minutes and 42 seconds, and the return flight to Los Angeles in three hours, 47 minutes and 39 seconds. Even on the last official flight of an SR-71 in January 1990 four speed records over set distances were broken. Contrary to its Soviet counterpart the MiG-25, (three to eight minutes at Mach 2.83), the SR-71 could maintain its top speed over long distances.

Speculation persists as to the reasons for decommissioning these complex aircraft but it may be assumed that they could not compete on a reasonable cost/use basis against satellite technology.

Between 1972 and 1989 the SR-71 flew 17,300 times, of these 3,551 were reconnaissance missions. (Ross NASA)

Selfie of SR-71 pilot Brian Shul during a reconnaissance flight at around 25,000 metres altitude. (Shul/USAF)

Lockheed S-3A *Viking*

Aircraft Type:	Lockheed S3-Viking
Purpose:	Maritime reconnaissance and ASW aircraft
Crew:	4
Engine:	2 x GE-TF34-400B turbofans
Wingspan:	20.92 m
Length:	16.26 m
Height:	6.93m
Wing surface:	55.55 m²
Top speed:	835 km/hr
Cruising speed:	650 km/hr
Max. rate of climb:	26 m/s
Service ceiling:	12,465 m
Range:	5,560 km

In 1967 the US Navy tendered for the design of a suitable updated successor to the ageing ASW Grumman S-2 Tracker. Lockheed submitted plans for its model S-3 Viking and emerged the clear winner. The advantages of the S-3 were clear to the Defence Ministry and Navy: compared to the S-2 Tracker it could reconnoitre an area three times the size and carry double the weaponry and sonobuoys. On 1 August 1967 the US Defence Ministry awarded Lockheed a US$461 million contract to build initially six experimental machines and three airframes. The maiden flight by the first of a total of eight testing machines took place on 21 January 1972 piloted by Lyle Schaefer and John Christiansen. The Viking was accepted by VS-41 Squadron on 20 February 1974.

The S-3 was a carrier-capable aircraft for long-range reconnaissance and anti-submarine warfare. Standard equipment included a 5-metre long MAD

(magnetic anomaly detector) extensible outrigger at the rear, an installation for launching sonobuoys on the fuselage floor, an internal weapons bay, and infra-red sensors below the cockpit. As a rule the crew of

The S-3A was a carrier-capable aircraft for long-range reconnaissance and anti-submarine warfare. (USN)

Standard equipment included a 5-metre long MAD (magnetic anomaly detector) extensible outrigger at the rear. (USN)

The crew of an S-3B Viking make the last preparations for take-off. (USN)

Compared to the S-2 Tracker, the Lockheed S-3A Viking could reconnoitre an area three times the size and carry double the weaponry and sonobuoys. (Lockheed-Martin)

187 S-3A Vikings were produced in five variants, and saw service with 14 squadrons of the US Navy. (USN)

The S-3A Viking could be refuelled in flight, a probe for the purpose being installed above the cockpit. (Stephens/ USN)

Like all aircraft designed to operate from aircraft carriers, the Viking fleet had a corresponding undercarriage with arrester-hook at the rear. (Franklin/USN)

For ease of stowage aboard ship the wings and very large vertical stabilizer could be folded. (McKiernan)

Four S-A3s fly for the Glenn Research Centre at NASA. (NASA)

the Viking was four men, seated in a climatized pressure cabin with ejector seats. The seating for pilot and co-pilot was located in the forward part of the cabin, the sensors-operator faced a work console at the cabin rear left side, and the tactical coordinator, responsible for the planning and execution of operations against enemy submarines, was at the right side. Because the Viking had been designed to operate from aircraft carriers, the machines had a corresponding undercarriage with arrester-hook at the rear. For ease of stowage aboard ship the wings and very large vertical stabilizer could be folded. The aircraft could be refuelled in flight, a probe for the purpose being installed above the cockpit.

187 of the type were produced in five variants, and saw service with 14 squadrons of the US Navy. The S-3 was officially decommissioned by the Navy from anti-submarine hunter squadron VS-22 on 29 January 2009, but four machines continue operational from the Pacific Missile Range Facility at Barking Sands on the Hawaiian island of Kauai for maritime reconnaissance: four other machines fly for the Glenn Research Centre at NASA.

Northrop Grumman E-8 *Joint STARS*

At the beginning of the 1980s, the US Air Force and Army acting jointly required a counterpart to the AWACS E-3 Sentry. The stated aim was to develop a so-called flying headquarters and command centre for all units specializing in operations against ground units. The result of years of development work was finally the Northrop Grumman E-8 JointSTARS for which, as with the E-3, the proven Boeing 707 was the godfather. The main characteristic of the E-8 is the 12-m long radar dome on the underside of the fuselage ahead of the wings. The E-8 radar is phase-guided and able to recognize and record movements of troops and material at a range of up to 250 kilometres – independent of the weather and far from the threat of the enemy. The data gathered is evaluated by 18 operators on the main deck and forwarded encrypted direct from the aircraft in real time to USAF command centres for closer evaluation and before transmission to friendly forces. While to a certain extent still in the testing stage, in 1991 the first two E-8s flew around 50 missions during *Desert Storm* over Iraq and Kuwait in the Second Gulf War and in reconnoitring Iraqi ground troops the aptness

of the machines for the role was found convincing. At present the USAF has over 17 of these machines, they are attached to Air Combat Command and based at the Robins air force base, Georgia.

Aircraft Type:	Northrop Grumman E-8 JointSTARS
Purpose:	Flying HQ and command centre
Crew:	4 flight crew and 18 operators
Engine:	4 x Pratt & Whitney TF33-102C turbofans, each 8540 kg thrust
Wingspan:	44.42 m
Length:	46.61 m
Height:	12.9 m
Wing surface:	283 m²
Top speed:	973 km/hr
Cruising speed:	945 km/hr
Max. rate of climb:	8.7 m/s
Service ceiling:	12,802 m
Range:	9,270 km

The main characteristic of the E-8 is the 12-m long radar dome on the underside of the fuselage ahead of the wings. (USAF)

The USAF has over 17 of these machines. They are attached to Air Combat Command and based at the Robins air force base, Georgia. (USAF)

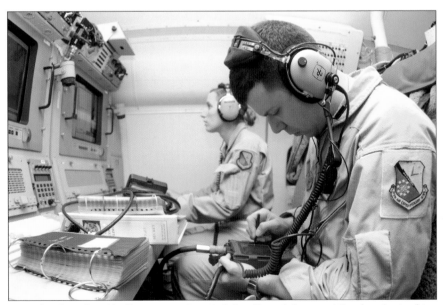

Data gathered is evaluated by 18 operators on the main deck and forwarded encrypted direct from the aircraft in real time to USAF command centres. (Beste/USAF)

Northrop Grumman RQ-4 *Global Hawk*

Shortly after sunrise on 28 February 1998 at the Edwards air force base 100 km north of Los Angeles, a strange aircraft rose into the cloudless sky. Softly and silent as a glider it sailed over nearby Antelope Valley and soon disappeared behind it. For the inhabitants of the region it was nothing out of the ordinary, for they are treated almost daily to the sight of aircraft never to be seen anywhere else so close up and so often. These are the test aircraft of the USAF kept secret from the general public. In this case however something peculiar was of note. It was seen from an amateur video that there was no cockpit or windows. For a while the machine remained a mystery, and not until much later was it discovered to be a prototype of an unmanned drone, the RQ-4 Global Hawk built by Northrop Grumman. Some 16 years later the machine, which cost US$30 million to build, is no longer a State secret but the world's largest series-built unmanned aircraft with a flight endurance of 40 hours and capable of operating worldwide with

Aircraft Type:	Northrop Grumman RQ-4B Global Hawk
Purpose:	Long range reconnaissance
Crew:	Unmanned
Engine:	1 x Rolls Royce Allison AE3007H turbofan
Wingspan:	39.89 m
Length:	14.50 m
Height:	4.63 m
Wing surface:	n/a
Top speed:	637 km/hr
Cruising speed:	637 km/hr
Max. rate of climb:	n/a
Service ceiling:	19,811 m
Range:	Endurance max.36 hrs=over 20,000 km

The drone RQ-4 Global Hawk cost around US$30 million to build and is the world's largest series-built unmanned aircraft. (Zapka/USAF)

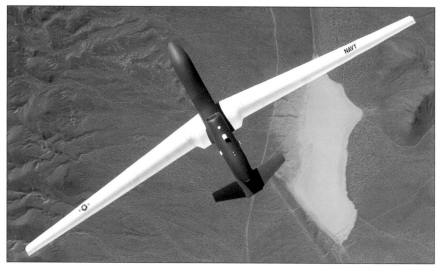

The RQ-4 is of aluminium bodywork, the wings and tailplane being of compound materials. (Gordon)

satellite support. It is remote-controlled as if it were an commercial aircraft with take-off, flight path and landing programmed into the flight computer. The pilot is on the ground, linked in directly via satellite and data radio to the drone's onboard system, and like any airborne pilot aboard a civilian airliner can make the drone change course as desired.

The RQ-4 is of aluminium bodywork, the wings and tailplane being of compound materials. With high definition infra-red sensitive CDD cameras for day and night vision and all-weather panoramic radar, the RQ-4 can recognize any object from around 20,000 metres altitude and cover an area of around 132,000 km^2 within 24 hours. The Global Hawk is

Since the end of 2011 the USAF has had a total of six RQ-4B drones officially in service. (Knott/USAF)

With the help of the RQ-4 atmospheric researchers will be able to closely investigate for the first time the upper troposphere and lower stratosphere. (NASA)die untere Stratosphäre. (NASA)

also capable of locating precisely the spot from where the weakest radio signal is being sent, can eavesdrop mobile telephone, intercept SMS text messages and cut into radio and television broadcasts. Similar to an electronic vacuum cleaner the drone's sensors are able to re-transmit the most diverse sources of emission in the form of electro-magnetic information through three different radio links for reception almost in real time by the ground station where the data is evaluated in the closest scientific detail.

In order to know the position of the drone at any given time, it is fitted with a standard navigational system and a differential GPS. Propulsion is by a Rolls-Royce turbofan also fitted in the regional commercial aircraft Embraer ERJ-145.

At present the RQ-4B (maiden flight 1 March 2007), the enlarged and further-developed version of the A-series is replacing the last remaining machines of the high-altitude reconnaissance aircraft Lockheed U-2. Since the end of 2011 the USAF has had a total of six RQ-4B drones in service officially.

Meanwhile meteorologists have also recognized how useful drones are in the collection of important

scientific information. In the early hours of 7 April 2010 a NASA Global Hawk of the Dryden Flight Research Centre at Edwards Air Force base took off with a special task. In the framework of Mission Global Hawk Pacific 2010, GloPac for short, a joint project between NASA and the National Oceanic and Atmospheric Administration (NOAA), an RQ-4 enabled atmospheric researchers to closely investigate for the first time the upper troposphere and lower stratosphere, an area largely inaccessible previously which lies between 5 kms and 20 kms altitude and is of enormous importance for research into climate change. The unmanned aircraft number 872 is one of three NASA reconnaissance drones. On board are eleven highly sensitive measuring instruments including spectographs able to detect without difficulty pollutants and toxic agents such as nitrous oxide, ozone- and suspended particles, and a gas chromatograph for the detection of hothouse gases. Other instruments search for important atmospheric components such as humidity or the KCKW gases which attack ozone. On this mission RQ-4 flew 20,000 kms from the Equator in the south to 85° of

In the early hours of 7 April 2010 a NASA Global Hawk of the Dryden Flight Research Centre at Edwards Air Force base took off with a special mission.

On board are eleven highly sensitive measuring instruments. (NASA)

latitude North and to Hawaii in the West. Co-workers at the Earth Science Division of NASA are impressed by the drone's endurance which from now on will allow them to reach polar regions and remote areas of ocean which entail risk for manned missions with a maximum period in the air of twelve hours.

Incidentally the RQ-4A also set some world records. The first was on a flight beginning on 21 March 2001 lasting 30 hours 24 minutes in which a drone flew a round course southwards along the Pacific coast and overflew Mexico, Central- and the northern part of South America at an altitude of 19,870 m. One month later on 23 April 2001 broke another world record by crossing the Pacific Ocean to Australia.

The newest variant still under development is the MQ-4C Triton for the US Navy for the monitoring of sea areas within the framework of the Broad Area Maritime Surveillance Program. It is planned to acquire 22 drones of this series.

Grumman S-2 *Tracker*/WF/E-1 *Tracer*

The career of the Grumman S-2 Tracker began in the Second World War. At that time the US Navy searched with so-called hunter-killer teams for enemy U-boats using sonar for detection purposes and then attacking with torpedoes and depth charges. These measures proved unsuitable postwar, for a new generation of nuclear-powered submarines was under development which were much faster and could dive deeper. Therefore the US Navy required an advanced alternative. Grumman learned of this need and developed the prototype for a combined maritime reconnaissance/ASW aircraft G-89 which had its maiden flight on 4 December 1952 and soon found the approval of the US Navy. The first series version under the official designation S-2A Tracker was adopted in February 1954 by the Anti-submarine Squadron V-26. More than 500 machines of this model were produced for the Navy and others exported to over 16 States including Argentina, Canada, Japan and the Netherlands.

Aircraft Type:	Grumman S-2E
Purpose:	Maritime reconnaissance and ASW
Crew:	4
Engine:	2 x Wright R-1820-82WA radials (2 x 1.137 kW/1,525 hp)
Wingspan:	22.12 m
Length:	13.26 m
Height:	5.33 m
Wing surface:	45.06 m²
Top speed:	450 km/hr
Cruising speed:	240 km/hr
Max. rate of climb:	n/a
Service ceiling:	6,700 m
Range:	2,170 km

More than 500 Grumman E-2 Tracker machines were produced for the US Navy. (US Navy)

Because the Tracker was intended to be carrier-capable, the aircraft was given folding wings and an arrester hook. (US Navy)

The S-2 Tracker was built as a high-wing monoplane since this guaranteed the greatest possible cabin volume. Also included was a large weapons bay, search radar in an adjustable under-fuselage tunnel and magnetic anomaly detector (MAD) in an extensible outrigger at the rear. Because the Tracker was intended to be carrier-capable, the aircraft was given folding wings and an arrester hook.

16 different versions of the S-2 were created during its career, the last used by the US Navy being the S-2G, a modifed version of the S-2E with modern ECM equipment. The S-2E and S-2G remained in service until the mid-1970s and were later replaced by the Lockheed S-3 Viking. Later on, Canada converted numerous S-2 Tracker aircraft to fire-fighters equipped with a 3,296-litre water tank, and Marsh Aviation still uses the S-2 to fight forest fires occurring in the Californian woodlands.

A further well-known variant based on the S-2 Tracker was the first carrier-borne early-warning aircraft Grumman E-1 Tracer, based on the Grumman C-1 Trader which was itself a development based on the S-2 Tracker. The E-1Tracer flew for the first time on 1 March 1957 and was in service with the US Navy a year later. Like the S-2, the Tracer was a high-wing monoplane with two radial engines, the gondolas also housing the undercarriage train. On the upper side of the fuselage the E-1 Tracer bore a rotatable radar dome containing the aerial of an AN/

The Tracker was exported to over 16 States including Argentina, Canada, Japan and the Netherlands. (Balcer)

A well-known variant of the S-2 Tracker was the first carrier-borne early-warning aircraft Grumman E-1 Tracer. (McKiernan)

On the upper side of the fuselage the E-1 Tracer bore a rotatable radar dome containing the aerial of an AN/APS-82 radar having a range of 320 kms. (McKiernan)

APS-82 radar having a range of 320 kms. This rotodome had a diameter of 5.12 metres and was 1.52 metres thick and could be revolved six times per minute.

As from 1970 the E-1 Tracer was gradually replaced by the Grumman E-2C Hawkeye. Its last operational use was aboard the USS Roosevelt in 1977 with reserve squadron RVAW-110 Firebirds. 88 Tracer machines were built.

Grumman E-2 *Hawkeye*

Aircraft Type:	Grumman E-2C Haweye
Purpose:	Early-warning and operational command aircraft
Crew:	5
Engine:	2 x Allison T-55-A-425 turbo-props
Wingspan:	24.56 m
Length:	17.54 m
Height:	5.58 m
Wing surface:	65.03 m²
Top speed:	602 km/hr
Cruising speed:	499 km/hr
Max. rate of climb:	n/a
Service ceiling:	9,390 m
Range:	2,855 km

The airborne early warning system had been developed in the Second World War. In the mid-1950s the first ideas were worked on for maintaining surveillance on airspace with specially equipped aircraft. Because Grumman had been involved in the development of the system from the beginning, it was only logical that the first aircraft with this function should come from the Grumman house – the Grumman E-1B Tracer. Its successor, the Grumman E-2 Hawkeye was not only the first carrier-capable aircraft in this role but was also the first aircraft conceived from the outset as a flying military headquarters. The design was for a twin-engined propellor aircraft with a five-man crew, the aircraft supporting on the top of its fuselage mid-section a General Electric AN/APS-96 radar in a rotating dome of 7.32 metres diameter. In order to combat the effects of this structure on flight stability, a wide tailplane with four fins and two rudders was found necessary.

The US Navy Squadron VAW-11 received the first of 62 machines on 19 January 1964, and over the course of the years the E-2 Hawkeye replaced more and more E-1s and became in the course of its career "The Fleet's Eye". (Leatherwood/USAF)

The E-2 had its baptism of fire at the end of 1965 in the Vietnam War and since then has served in all theatres of war worldwide in which US aircraft carriers have participated. (USN)

The aircraft are used in teams of two or more at an operational height of around 9,000 metres.

The APS-125 radar of the E-2C is able to detect even over land difficult to spot flying objects up to a range of 370 km.

Hawkeye operations are made as a rule from aircraft carriers. (USN)

The first prototype W2F-1 took off on its maiden flight on 21 October 1960. The US Navy Squadron VAW-11 received the first of 62 machines on 19 January 1964, and over the course of the years the E-2 replaced more and more E-1s and soon became "The Eye of the Fleet". The E-2 had its baptism of fire in 1965 in Viet Nam and since then has served in all theatres of war worldwide in which US aircraft carriers have participated. In 1969 all operational E-2As were brought up to the E-2B standard with improved computer technology and air-refuelling capability. The aircraft are used in teams of two or more at an operational height of around 9,000 metres.

In the summer of 1971 Grumman began producing the E-2C with modified avionics: this version was commissioned by VAW-123 in November 1973. The E-2C was exported to Israel (4), Japan (8), Egypt (2), Singapore (4) and elsewhere. The APS-125 radar of the E-2C, developed in common by General Electric and Grumman, is also able to detect over land difficult to spot flying objects up to a range of 370 km. Furthermore there is an option using data processing materials aboard to pursue automatically and simultaneously 250 objects and conduct in parallel 30 intercept operations. The data is evaluated on board by three systems officers and transmitted in

real time to the forces below. The E-2C is also equipped with a passive sensor system (PDS) which reports automatically the presence, direction of travel and identity of every object up to a range of 800 km. At present the probably last variants of the E-2 are operational, the E-2D Advanced Hawkeye, based on the further developed C-series Hawkeye 2000 as from the year 2000 and which has for the first time the new rotatable APY-9 active electronic scanned array and improved communications electronics. The E-2D Delta One flew for the first time on 3 August 2007. The US Navy has announced that it has a present requirement for 75 of this Type. Hawkeye operations are made as a rule from aircraft carriers.

In 1962 the Navy decided on a carrier-supply version (COD-Carrier Onboard Delivery), and initially ordered three such machines designated C-2A Greyhound, the first prototype of which absolved its maiden flight on 18 November 1964. In all, 25 of these machines were built, similar in structure to the E-2 but without the radar cupola. The V-shape of the tailplane was also redesigned, and the aircraft now has more space for crew, passengers and cargo. In the course of its career, the Grumman C-2A played an important role in delivering supplies to US aircraft carriers.

View into the cockpit of an E-2C during an operational flight over the Pacific. (USN)

The design was for a twin-engined propellor aircraft with a five-man crew, the aircraft supporting on the top of its fuselage mid-section a General Electric AN/APS-96 radar in a rotating dome of 7.32 metres diameter. (Poplin/USN)

The data is evaluated on board by three systems officers and transmitted in real time to the forces below. (USN)

Kawasaki P-1

The Kawasaki P-1 is a maritime surveillance aircraft with Anti-Submarine Warfare capability. Its development was begun in Japan in 2001. The maiden flight was on 28 September 2007 from the Gifu AF base. The P-1 is a low-wing monoplane with four IHI (Ishikkawajima-Harima-Heavy Industries) XF7-10 turbofans. The aircraft is fitted with the most modern anti-submarine system worldwide which supplies the pilots with the best course for attack based on the target's current movements. Steering is Fly-by-Light (a very modern, optic-electronic technology) which has the advantage over the Fly-by-Wire system that electro-magnetic interference is substantially reduced. This is often of decisive importance since the detection of submarines is based on measurements of the magnetic field. Also available to the crew is radar with active electronic scanned array (AESA) and an infrared/video search system.

Aircraft Type:	Kawasaki P-1
Purpose:	Maritime surveillance and ASW
Crew:	2 flying personnel + 12 operators
Engine:	4 x IHI-XF7-10 turbofan each of 5,000 kg thrust
Wingspan:	35 m
Length:	38 m
Height:	12 m
Wing surface:	n/a
Top speed:	900 km/hr
Cruising speed:	830 km/hr
Max. rate of climb:	n/a
Service ceiling:	13,520 m
Range:	8,000 km

Over the coming years the Japanese Navy is planning to buy a fleet of 80 of these aircraft for US$140 million each.

The Kawasaki P-1 has the most modern ASW system in the world. Over the next few years the Japanese Navy is planning to buy a fleet of 80 of these aircraft at a cost of US$140 million each.

Avro 696 *Shackleton*

Aircraft Type:	Avro 696 Shackleton MR3
Purpose:	Maritime reconnaissance
Crew:	10
Engine:	4 x 12-cylinder-Rolls Royce Griffon 57A V-motors each 1,831 kW.
Wingspan:	36.52 m
Length:	28.19 m
Height:	7.11 m
Wing surface:	132 m²
Top speed:	480 km/hr
Cruising speed:	n/a
Max. rate of climb:	n/a
Service ceiling:	5,669 m
Range:	4,260 km

When enquiries in Great Britain for long-range maritime reconnaissance aircraft increased, the development of the Lincoln III was suggested for this role in 1946.

The Avro 694 Lincoln had already distinguished itself in the Second World War as an improved version of the Lancaster for Pacific operations with greater range and heavier armament. With Rolls-Royce Merlin engines the aircraft was called Lancaster IV, with Packard Merlin engines Lancaster V. In order to avoid confusion the names were changed to Lincoln I and II respectively.

Avro's comprehensive new design Lincoln III was given the name Shackleton after the polar explorer Ernest Shackleton. The aircraft kept the Lincoln wings and undercarriage but was given a completely new fuselage, shorter but of larger cross-section. The tailplane was raised and the characteristic fins of the Lancaster/Lincoln were now rounder and heavier. The Merlin motors were replaced by four Rolls-Royce Griffon motors each driving a pair of contra-rotating, three-bladed propellors. The new fuselage was large enough to accommodate a crew of ten, 2 x 20-mm cannons, (one on either side of the nose), two more 20-mm cannons and 2 x 12.7-mm MG's in the rear gunner's turret plus bombs or depth charges in a large floor section. The machine was now designated Shackleton GR1, later changed to Shackleton MR1. The maiden flight was made on 24 October 1950, the aircraft was adopted in February 1951 by 120 Squadron RAF and by No.236 OCU (Operational Conversion Unit) at Kinloss, and later replaced the Lancaster MR.III in the Coastal Command squadrons.

The MR.1 Griffon initially served the 57A inner and Griffon 57 outer motors, the second series production were all Griffon 57A motors with broader gondolas for the outer motors and given the designation Shackleton MR.1A. The MR.1-series soon proved trouble-prone. The radar installation was of limited usefulness and the armament positioned at

All earlier versions of the Shackleton were replaced by the Nimrod MR.1/2 from 1991. (Ruth)

Avro's comprehensive new design of the Lincoln III was named Shackleton after the polar explorer Ernest Shackleton. (Lopez/USAF) Ernest Shackleton. (Lopez/USAF)

the nose and tail were not effective resulting in the quick development of the Shackleton MR.II with new streamlined front section and twin 20-mm cannons above the bomb-aimer's position. The nose radar was dismounted and replaced by a partially retractable "Dustbin" aerial with 360° sweep in a radome behind the bomb bay: the rear-gunner's turret gave way to a cone-shaped look-out position, and a retractable double tail wheel supplanted the former fixed single tail wheel.

The final series, Shackleton MR.III, was generally of better overall performance with redesigned wings and rudders, wingtip tanks, transparent cabin roof and a soundproof crewroom for a second shift on long patrols. This increase in weight required a retractable nose wheel and a doubling-up of the main undercarriage wheels. The most noticeable outward modification was the removal of the pulpit turret to make way for materials. The South African Air Force took eight of the 42 series models. All earlier versions of the Shackleton were replaced by the Nimrod MR.1/2 from 1991. The last variant was the AEW.2 (Airborne Early Warning) system developed by British Aerospace from 1972 as an alternative to the Fairey/Westland Gannet AEW.3 which had no seaborne base after the Royal Navy decommissioned its last aircraft carrier. A total of twelve Type MR.2 were converted into AEW.2 machines, the partially retractable "Dustbin" aerials being replaced by fixed Guppy aerials just ahead of the weapons station, this variant had an APS-20 radar search device as aboard the Gannet plus seating and consoles for three radio operators.

British Aerospace (HS) *Nimrod MR*

Within the framework of Operational Requirement 381 at the beginning of the 1960s, the RAF ordered a maritime reconnaissance aircraft primarily to keep watch on Soviet submarines. It was planned that this aircraft would also replace the meanwhile obsolescent Avro Shackleton. The basis for the model was the de Havilland Comet 4C. The fuselage with its circular cross-section was retained but shortened by 1.98 metres, and a non-pressurized lower part added to the fuselage for the search radar and behind it a spacious weapons bay and locations for various other systems. The basic model was fitted with four efficient Rolls-Royce RB 168 turbofan jets (with reverse thrust for the outer pair), these were especially economic on fuel at low altitude: wingtip tanks with a searchlight in the right tank, a passive French ESM-receiver as an electronic support measure in a gondola at the upper edge of the tail fin and a MAD (maritime anomaly detector) in a long projection at the extreme rear. The machine also received new radar systems and sensors for maritime reconnaissance. The first of two prototypes flew for the first time in May 1967. The 46 Nimrod MR.1 machines ordered by the RAF were made operational at RAF Kinloss in October 1969. Up to 1974 a further 45 of the Type had been delivered, the last of them from the Nimrod Mk 2 series. By

Aircraft Type:	British Aerospace (HS) Nimrod MR
Crew:	13
Engine:	4 x Rolls Royce RB 168-20 turbofan each of 5400 kg thrust
Wingspan:	35 m
Length:	38.63 m
Height:	9.14 m
Wing surface:	197.05 m²
Top speed:	923 km/hr
Cruising speed:	787 km/hr
Max. rate of climb:	n/a
Service ceiling:	12,800 m
Range:	9,254 km

1979 the overall fleet had been upgraded to the Nimrod Mk 2 standard, the machines being fitted with a new tactical system, computer, installations to analyze radar and acoustic signals, upgraded telecommunications system, inertial navigation, new instruments and steering controls and crew training facilities.

The basis for the first Nimrod was the de Havilland Comet 4C. The first of two prototypes absolved the maiden flight in May 1967. (Chris Lofting)

The first version was fitted with four efficient Rolls-Royce RB 168 turbofan jets with reverse thrust. (Pingstone)

Because the machines were often over twelve hours in the air they were fitted with equipment for mid-air refuelling. (Wilson)

The first frontline operations occurred in 1982 during the Falklands War. Because the machines were often over twelve hours in the air they were fitted with equipment for mid-air refuelling.

As a rule the Nimrod crew consisted of two pilots and an engineer on the flight deck, tactical navigators, two sonar operators, a radar and ESM/MAD technician and two loaders. The latter loaded and launched active or passive sonobuoys or sea markers through the shafts at the rear of the aircraft and kept watch for enemy shipping through the curved windows of the aircraft. Between 1990 and 2009 the Nimrod fleet took part in land reconnaissance operations during the conflicts in the

As a rule the Nimrod flight crew consisted of two pilots and an engineer. (Brown/RAF)

Between 1990 and 2009 the Nimrod fleet took part in land reconnaissance operations during the conflicts in the Middle East, and between 1992 and 1997 above Yugoslavia. (Hannan/USAF)

Middle East, and between 1992 and 1997 above Yugoslavia.

From 1974 the RAF deployed three Nimrods as strategic patrol aircraft. The machines given the suffix R-1 were fitted for both SIGINT- and ELINT-reconnaissance. Their purpose was to obtain important information regarding Soviet communications traffic and movements of troops and submarines in all States of the Eastern bloc. Unlike the MR1 and MR2, the R-1 carried no armament and was Britain's best-kept secret during the Cold War. Not until 1994 was its existence confirmed. Even today the Nimrod R-1 is considered the most modern aircraft of this kind outside the United States. A further planned version was the Nimrod AEW3.Mk 3 intended primarily for AWACS operations but this

project was abandoned in favour of the Boeing E-3 Sentry in 1987. The same fate befell the new generation Nimrod MRA4 which were to have replaced a large segment of the MR 2 fleet compared to which it was virtually a totally new design. The MRA4 was given larger wings, and new Rolls-Royce turbofan engines for longer range at less operating cost. The maiden flight was held on 10 September 2009. The British Government was planning to acquire twelve machines of this series, but the project was cancelled for budgetary reasons. In 2010 after 13 years all converted aircraft were decommissioned, the SIGINT-version a year later.

The circular cross-section of the Nimrod fuselage. (King)

Dassault-Breguet Br.1150 *Atlantic*

The tensions in the East-West relationship reached a new height at the beginning of the 1950s. The Cold War was having its effect; the Soviet Union armed against the West and the threat from Soviet submarines, operating in the North Atlantic and equipped with ICBM's, caused NATO increasing concerns. In April 1957 the NATO partners set up a team of experts to decide what kind of modern maritime reconnaissance and anti-submarine warfare was required. On 2 March 1958 the NATO aviation industry received the catalogue of specifications with a request that work on such project should begin forthwith, and subsequently a total of 26 firms submitted 21 projects in response to the tender. Three were short-listed and on 21 October 1958 Breguet's model Br.1150 emerged the winner. The contracts to develop the machine were signed on 7 December 1959 with SECBAT (Sociéte Européene pour la Construction du Breguet Atlantic), the consortium set up for the purpose by Breguet, and the financing of the project in common was split between West Germany (19.1%), Belgium (7.8%), Netherlands (15.3%) and France (57.8%).

Aircraft Type:	Dassault-Breguet Br.1150 Atlantic Nimrod MR
Purpose:	Maritime reconnaissance and ASW.
Crew:	12
Engine:	2 x Rolls Royce SNECMA Type Mk.21
Wingspan:	36.30 m
Length:	31.75 m
Height:	11.30m
Wing surface:	120.34 m²
Top speed:	658 km/hr
Cruising speed:	500 km/hr
Max. rate of climb:	12.5 m/sec
Service ceiling:	10,000 m
Range:	7,677 km

The Br.1150 Atlantic is a twin-engined mid-wing monoplane of all-metal hull construction. In cross-section the fuselage has the shape of a figure 8 and

The Breguet Atlantic is the only aircraft in the world designed and built specifically for the maritime reconnaissance role. (Bundeswehr/Marine)

The era of the Br.1150 ended for the German Navy on 20 June 2010 after more than 40 years. (Bundeswehr Marine)

the unique thing about this aircraft is that it is the only aircraft in the world designed and built specifically for the maritime reconnaissance role. Other long-range reconnaissance aircraft such as the Lockheed P-3 Orion for example started life as a rule as civilian aircraft.

The pressurized upper section contains the cockpit and flight deck, the work stations of the 12-man crew, galley, WC, restroom with bunks, an observation station and the main access door at the rear. In the non-pressurized lower section are the search radar, the 9-metre long shaft for torpedoes, depth charges and mines. The launch equipment for sonobuoys and a retro-cannon for light- and smoke-markers are located in the rear.

The basic design of the Atlantic is by Breguet, other partners were Sud Aviation, the Belgian manufacturer ABAP (Association Belge pour l'avion Patrouiller), the German "Seeflug" consortium of the firms Dornier and Siebel ATG founded in April 1962, Fokker from the Netherlands and from 1968 Aeritalia. The division of production arranged that ABAP would deliver the wing roots and landing flaps, Breguet the forward fuselage with pulpit and the central fuselage. The rear including the tailplane was produced by

Dornier and Siebel, the wing centre sections including the engine gondolas were supplied by Fokker. Sud Aviation completed the outer sections of wing, the maufacturer Aeritalia which joined later delivered the lower hull of the fuselage rear together with the access door, rudders and elevators. The final assembly and coordination of the project lay finally in the hands of Dassault-Breguet.

The maiden flight of the first Atlantic prototype Works Nr. 01 was made on 21 October 1961, and on 3 November the baptismal ceremony and official inauguration was held at Toulouse-Blagnac. The second prototype was flight-tested on 23 February 1962, but after 50 flights over southern France it crashed on a test flight on 19 April the same year. After the forward section of fuselage had been lengthened by 0.91 metres and the wing roots reinforced at mid-wing, the third prototype flew for the first time on 25 February 1963 fitted with the entire electronic equipment. The fourth prototype took off for its maiden flight on 10 September 1964. Besides these four prototypes an airframe was built for static and dynamic testing.

The order books were meanwhile well-filled led by France with 40 machines, then West Germany 20,

France was the major buyer of the Breguet Atlantic with its order for 40 machines of this Type. The photo shows a Br.1150 in the livery of the French Navy. (Cinelli/USN)

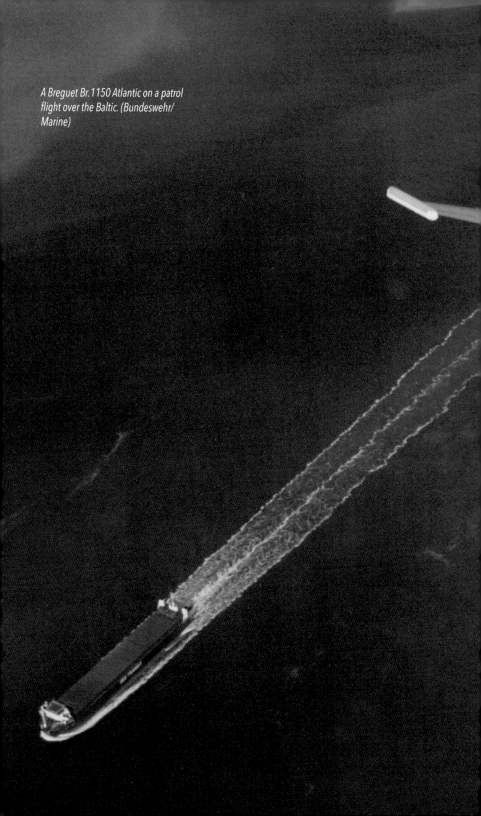

A Breguet Br.1150 Atlantic on a patrol flight over the Baltic. (Bundeswehr/Marine)

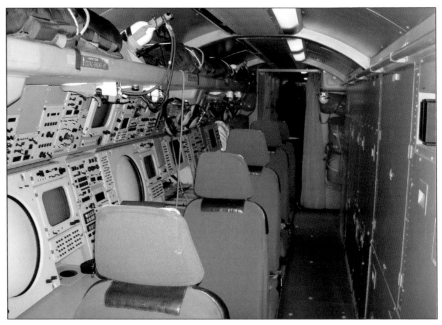

The pressurized upper section contains the cockpit, the work stations for the 12-man crew, galley, WC, restroom with bunks and observation station. (Wikimedia)

View into the cockpit of the Breguet Atlantic. (Wikimedia)

The Br.1150 Atlantic is a twin-engined mid-wing monoplane of all-metal hull construction, the fuselage cross-section has the shape of a figure 8. (Pingstone)

Italy 18 and Holland 9. On 15 July 1965 the first prototype arrived at the German naval air squadron MFG 3, Nordholz, and the French Navy received its first machine on 10 December.

In 1970 the French Navy planned the further development of the Atlantic Br. 1150 into the Atlantic ATL 2 with more modern equipment and weapons technology. In 1972 for that purpose SECBAT set up a modernization commission whose aim was to urge the Governments involved to arrange the corresponding work commission. However the relaxing of tension in East-West relationships convinced the French Government to reduce its fleet

from 42 machines to 20 while the upgrading project with its high cost for replacement parts and large labour force found little enthusiasm with the West German Navy. Eventually the Defence Ministries of Bonn and Rome decided that their existing fleets would be merely modernized. In 1978 Breguet proceeded with a development towards the ATL 2 by upgrading only the equipment of two machines of the first generation, and these had their maiden flight on 8 May 1981 and 26 March 1982 respectively. The era of the Br.1150 ended for the German Navy on 20 June 2010 after more than 35 years.

Raytheon
Sentinel R1

The Raytheon Sentinel R1 is an RAF reconnaissance aircraft developed especially to monitor the battlefield in Afghanistan. Its purpose is to detect small targets such as tanks or assault guns and follow their progress. The Sentinel R1 is a joint project between the manufacturers Raytheon Company and Bombardier Aerospace and is based on the successful executive jet Bombardier Global Express. The R1 is easily recognizable by its two prominent radar domes behind which is the Raytheon developed airborne battlefield radar ASARS-2. Decisive for the choice was probably the fact that this radar is also used by the British Army and Royal Navy. The R1 had its first maiden flight in May 2004 but the first machines were not delivered to 5.Squadron RAF at Weddington until three years later. Since 2008 five of these aircraft have been operational officially over Afgani airspace, and in the British Government's White Book all are due to be decommissioned once these particualar operations are concluded. The total operation is costing the British Government and taxpayer around a billion euros.

Since 2008 five of these aircraft have been operational officially over Afgani airspace monitoring the battlefield. (Radecki)

The two principal features of the R1 are the two large radar domes with the airborne battlefield radar ASARS-2. (Radecki)

Aircraft Type:	Raytheon Sebtinel R1
Purpose:	Reconnaissance aircraft
Crew:	5
Engine:	2 x Rolls Royce BR710 each of 6560 kgs thrust
Wingspan:	28.50 m
Length:	30.30 m
Height:	8.20m
Wing surface:	94.90 m²
Top speed:	950 km/hr
Cruising speed:	904 km/hr
Max. rate of climb:	n/a
Service ceiling:	14,935 m
Range:	9,250 km

Beriyev A-50 *Mainstay*/IL-82

Following extensive examination of the design by the official offices in May 1969, work on the first prototype of the Ilyushin-76 was begun by the Soviet design bureau G.W.Ilyushin under the leadership of Constructor-General Ghenrich Novoshilov at the beginning of 1970. Already on the drawing board the striking similarity of the design to the American Lockheed C-141A was noticeable – but the IL-76 is much heavier and more powerful. It cannot transport large payloads, and does not have the same great range as its American counterpart but it can – as no other comparable aircraft of its size – operate from short rough runways and above all in bad weather conditions. Another novelty which can be attributed to the IL-76 is the fact that the aircraft is faster, more economic and also requires less maintenance that comparable types of the same age. Within the

framework of experimental studies, the aircraft carried a 40-tonne payload over a distance of 5,000 kms in less than six hours. Naturally, this

Aircraft Type:	Beriyev A-50
Purpose:	Airspace reconnaissance aircraft
Crew:	16
Engine:	4 x Aviadvigatel PS-90A-turbofan each 1570 kg thrust
Wingspan:	50.54 m
Length:	47.50 m
Height:	14.76 m
Wing surface:	300 m²
Top speed:	765 km/hr
Cruising speed:	n/a
Max. rate of climb:	n/a
Service ceiling:	10,200 m
Range:	7,300 km

Towards the mid-1970's, Beriyev developed the AWACS reconnaissance Beriyev A-50 Mainstay on the elongated fuselage of the IL-76. (Wilson)

The WEGA-M Schmel radar apparatus has a range of around 800 metres and can identify and track up to 200 targets at the same time. (Doomych)

Besides Russia, the Indian Army also operates the A-50. (Sender)

The A-50 can keep flying in its operational area for up to six hours without refuelling. (Kazachkov)

capability pre-destined the IL-76 for military work.

To a certain extent a replacement for the Tupolev Tu-126, towards the mid-1970s, the Beriyev team led by Alexei Konstantinov developed the AWACS reconnaissance Beriyev A-50 Mainstay on the elongated fuselage of the IL-76. The A-50 flew for the first time in 1980 but delivery of the first series machines and its commissioning into the aerial forces had to wait until the mid-1980s. It is estimated that in 1990 there were around twelve of these machines operational. Essentially the method of working, the function and the operating spectrum of the A-50 is identical to, and comparable with, the Boeing E-3 Sentry and other AWACS machines. Similarly the most important characteristic of the A-50 is the dorsal radome housing the WEGA-M Schmel radar apparatus which has a range of around 800 metres and can identify and track up to 200 targets at the same time. As with the Boeing Sentry, the primary objective of the A-50 is to reconnoitre airspace. For this purpose the A-50 can keep flying in its operational area for up to six hours without refuelling. Another of its roles is as a so-called flying command centre used to coordinate allied units, as a

The IL-82 is used to direct the Russian atomic submarine fleet and also serves as a flying Command HQ. (Wilson)

rule with the aid of satellite communications. Besides Russia, the A-50 is also used by the Indian Army.

Also based on the IL-76 is the IL-82, the most imposing element of which is the radar bulge with Satcom-/Infrared equipment positioned on the roof just aft of the cockpit.

Amongst other roles, the IL-82 is used to direct the Russian atomic submarine fleet and would also serve as a flying Command HQ in the event of nuclear attack. Some sources report that, like the IL-86 VPK, the IL-82 was deployed as an early warning aircraft at the time of the Cold War. There is speculation that still only one machine is operational. Of further interest is the paintwork in the colours of the civilian Russian airline Aeroflot, apparently for camouflage purposes.

Ilyushin IL-20

In 1970 the threat from increasingly more modern ICBM's necessitated the development of ever more modern reconnaissance aircraft which would also be able to eavesdrop even the smallest details of information from opposing forces. Aircraft manufacturers on both sides saw themselves facing a great challenge. In the area of espionage and reconnaissance at the beginning of the Cold War the Soviet Union at least had had only moderate success. The Soviets lacked the necessary know-how and infrastructure. Both shortcomings caused such disquiet to the Government in Moscow that they ordered a reconnaissance aircraft which matched up to its Western counterparts in efficiency and technology. The robust and powerful passenger aircraft IL-18 seemed suitable for the task, and so the manufacturer Ilyushin decided that numerous IL-18 withdrawn from civilian service would be subjected to comprehensive conversion measures to bring them up to the standard of ECM- and ELINT-aircraft for electronic espionage and warfare. These machines were given the designation IL-20, but up to the present only scant information as to their capability and flight electronics workings has become available. Unconfirmed reports suggest that they corresponded

Aircraft Type:	Ilyushin IL-20M
Purpose:	Reconnaissance aircraft
Crew:	c.4
Engine:	4 x Ivtchenko AL-20M turboprops each of 3,169 kW
Wingspan:	37.42 m
Length:	35.90 m
Height:	10.17 m
Wing surface:	140 m²
Top speed:	675 km/hr
Cruising speed:	n/a
Max. rate of climb:	n/a
Service ceiling:	10,000 m
Range:	6,500 km

approximately to that of the Boeing RC-135. The IL-20 was first seen by NATO partners in 1978, particularly around the British Isles. Striking characteristics of the machine are the torpedo-like feature beneath the fuselage – it is assumed that this might be a Side-Looking-Airborne-Radar (SLAR) used amongst other things for radar imagery and cartographic purporses – and the housing with two windows on each side of the fuselage above it which might be for infrared technology or simply to accommodate optical

The IL-20 is used inter alia *for electronic espionage/warfare. (Naumenko)*

The housing on the fuselage side might be for infrared technology. (Naumenko)

In 1967 four IL-18 were converted to IL-20RT/SIP able to follow the flight path of rockets and other missiles. (Krivchikov)

The IL-20 was first seen by NATO partners in 1978, particularly around the British Isles. (Zherdin)

sensors. Other features of note are the numerous small aerials for gathering electronic data and two large aerials on the fuselage rear upper side for satellite communications which make it possible to relay information in real time to ground stations.

In 1967 four IL-18 were converted to IL-20RT/SIP (SIP=Samolotny Ismeritelni Punkt, or Flying Measuring Point/Place). The operational spectrum of this machine is comparable with the Boeing EC-135 since one of the purposes of the IL-20RT is to follow the flight path of rockets and other missiles. For this reason the machines were given a dorsal radar bulge to house sensitive sensors and aerials. The aircraft were stationed at Leninsk near the Baikonur rocket station.

Ilyushin IL-38 *May*

In June 1960 upon instructions from the Central Committee and Superior Ministerial Counsellor, the Ilyushin organisation began work on the IL-38 long-range maritime reconnaissance and anti-submarine aircraft codenamed "May" by NATO. From the outset the development was headed by Sergei Ilyushin with Jakov Kooterov as his Chief Engineer. Like the IL-20, the IL-38 is based on the IL-18 but in contrast to the IL-18 has a 4-metres longer fuselage with the wings set 1.8 metres forward to compensate for the change in the centre of gravity caused by siting the electronic equipment towards the nose. Test pilot Vladimir Kokkinaki flew a prototype for the maiden flight on 28 September 1961, but the aircraft was not delivered to the Soviet maritime forces for a full eight years because of major problems with the avionics. Even after the aircraft was given the green light for series production in December 1965, the official commissioning of the IL-38 did not take place until 17 January 1969. The Soviet Central Committee and the Superior Counsellor were planning at one time a batch of 250 machines of this Type, but eventually

Aircraft Type:	Ilyushin IL-38 May
Purpose:	Long-range maritime reconnaissance and ASW aircraft
Crew:	10
Engine:	4 x Ivtchenko AL-20M turboprops each of 3,169 kW.
Wingspan:	37.42 m
Length:	40.07 m
Height:	10.10 m
Wing surface:	140 m^2
Top speed:	720 km/hr
Cruising/patrol speed:	350 km/hr
Max. rate of climb:	320 m/min
Service ceiling:	10,000 m
Range:	9,500 km

production terminated in 1972 after only 58 had been built. The aircraft were deployed by 24.OPAP at Severomorsk, by 77.OPAP at Nikolayeva near Vladivostok and by 145 OPAE at Riga.

The IL-38 was accepted officially into the Soviet forces on 17 January 1969. (Dvurekov)

Russia is planning to maintain its IL-38 fleet in service until at least 2020 at the Severomorsk, Petropavlovsk-Kamchatski and Nikolayeva bases. (USN)

An IL-38 overflying the aircraft carrier USS Midway. (USN)

An Ilyushin IL-38 over the Pacific on 10 October 1981 accompanied by a Vought A-7 Corsair from the aircraft carrier USS Coral Sea. (Kennedy/USN)

The Soviet Central Committee and Superior Counsellor once planned a batch of 250 of these machines. (USN)

In order to lengthen the period in the operational area, between 1974 and 1977 a variant designated IL-38M was tested with an air-refuelling probe, while another variant, the IL-38MZ, was tried out with an extensible refuelling hose stowed in the bomb-bay. Neither devices made it past the prototype stage and so both probably failed to reach the forces officially. On 4 April 2001 Ilyushin tested the modernized IL-38N. A significant feature of this version is a modern ELINT-system. In September 2001 the Russian Defence Ministry issued a US$200 million contract to modernize the fleet under the designation IL-38SD. The first examples of this series were delivered to the Russian forces from 2006, two of them went to the Indian Army. The Russian Defence Ministry is planning to maintain its IL-38 fleet in service until at least 2020 at the Severomorsk, Petropavlovsk-Kamchatski and Nikolayeva bases.

In 1983 Western aerial forces photographed the modified IL-38 May-B variant with additional radar dome below the fuselage. (USN)

Two examples of the IL-38SD went to the aerial forces of India. (Krivchikov)

Ilyushin IL-80 Maxdome

Aircraft Type:	Ilyushin IL-80
Crew:	c.20
Engine:	4 x Kuznetzov NK-86 each of 1275 kgs thrust.
Wingspan:	48.06 m
Length:	59.94 m
Height:	15.81 m
Wing surface:	320 m²
Top speed:	950 km/hr
Cruising/patrol speed:	900 km/hr
Max. rate of climb:	n/a
Service ceiling:	12,000 m
Range:	4,600 km

With a surface area of 17,075,400 km², an eighth of the world's land, Russia is the world's largest State. According to a census in May 2006, Russia has 142,500,000 inhabitants, and therefore on average every square kilometre of land has 8.3 inhabitants. Many land areas of Russia are so remote as to only be reachable by aircraft. As a result, passenger air traffic on the most important Soviet interior routes was correspondingly high, and soon the constantly increasing air traffic became a problem once aviation experts identified the number of take-offs and landings as a danger to airport safety. The cause of the problem and its solution were soon found: the former Soviet standard passenger aircraft Tupolev TU-154 and Ilyushin IL-62 only had accommodation for from 83 to 180 passengers. A further growth in aircraft numbers could only be impeded by building an aircraft to take more passengers. The result was presented in 1970 by the S.W.Ilyushin Design Bureau in the form of the huge passenger aircraft IL-86 of the third generation of civilian aircraft.

Air-based command centre IL-80 or IL-86 VKP was designed for the Soviet military and President in the case of a nuclear attack. (Beltyukov)

It is thought that the former Soviet armed forces once had five of these aircraft of which only three remain operational. (Naumenko)

The IL-80 is comparable to the western Boeing E-4B. (Kuzmin)

The IL-80 has no outer windows (save for the flight cabin) in order to protect the aircraft against the pressure wave of an atomic explosion and electro-magnetic impulses. (Beltyukov)

During the course of its history, the IL-86 was used not only for passenger services, but also for military purposes as a troop transport or later as an air-based command centre for the Soviet military and the President in the case of a nuclear attack. In this role the aircraft received the designation IL-80 or IL-86 VKP.

It is supposed that the former Soviet armed forces once had five of these aircraft of which only three were to be operational, all to be stationed with 8. Special Air Force Division at the Chkalovsky base about 30 kms north of Moscow.[1] Western photographs captured the IL-80 for the first time in 1992, but it is assumed that the machines had been in service with the former Soviet forces since the mid-1980s. The IL-80 has no outer windows (save for the flight cabin) in order to protect the aircraft against the pressure wave of an atomic explosion and electro-magnetic impulses. To judge by its role and method of operation the IL-80 is comparable to the Boeing E-4B. Also of interest here is the paintwork in the colours of the civilian Russian airline Aeroflot, apparently for camouflage purposes.

Note

1. On 6 August 2016 the Kremlin reported that its Security Council had ordered "the immediate deployment of two Doomsday aircraft" as a "defensive reaction" to certain events occurring internationally. These two aircraft were the Il-80 described here and a modified Il-96-400 wide bodied aircraft.

Myassishtev M-4A/C

After 1945 reconnaissance aircraft came into being not only in the West but also in the Soviet Union, as a rule developed from heavy long-range bombers since these had the necessary size and range. Additionally it was obviously more economic to develop and build different variants from a single model to suit the most varied operational purposes. A striking example from the Soviet Union is the strategic long-range bomber M-4 from the manufacturer Myassishtev. It is assumed today that it was built on Stalin's direct order. From 1924 Vladimir M. Myassishtev contributed a whole series of Soviet aircraft designs, but became best known for his meanwhile legendary M-4 – the first operational, four-engined, jet-turbine Soviet bomber which had its maiden flight on 20 January 1953 and was shown to the public for the first time at a display of aircraft on Red Square on 1 May 1954. The M-4 was built as a cantilever mid-wing monoplane with thick swept wings and swept tailplane. The undercarriage consisted of two main legs, positioned in tandem one behind the other

Aircraft Type:	Myassishtev M-4B/C
Purpose:	Long range bomber and maritime reconnaissance
Crew:	6-11 men
Engine:	4 x Mikulin AM3-D turbojets each of 8,560 kg thrust
Wingspan:	50.48 m
Length:	47.20 m
Height:	12.80 m
Wing surface:	309 m²
Top speed:	1,000 km/hr
Cruising/patrol speed:	900 km/hr
Max. rate of climb:	n/a
Service ceiling:	13,700 m
Range:	9,800 km

below the fuselage centre, each equipped with a four-wheel tandem axle. The gear also included retractable twin wheels to support the wing tips. For the crew the

The M-4 was shown to the public for the first time at a display of aircraft on Red Square in Moscow on 1 May 1954. (Schwede Archive)

The maritime reconnaissance version "Bison-B", first identified in 1964 by NATO forces, belongs amongst the later modified versions of the M-4. (Schwede Archive)

cylindrical fuselage had a pressure cabin forward and rotating turret at the rear. Integrated at the wing roots were four Mikulin AM-3D jet engines each with 8560 kgs thrust. The original bomber version, intended *inter alia* to carry nuclear weapons over intercontinental distances, had the codename "Bison-A" and according to unconfirmed reports was in Soviet service from 1954. Its size and purpose corresponded to that of the Boeing B-52. Amongst the later modified versions was the maritime reconnaissance aircraft "Bison-B", first identified by NATO forces in 1964 which had a massive nose with radome in place of the glazed nose, and a refuelling probe directly above the cockpit. The Bison-B was also one of the first Soviet aircraft which could be refuelled

in flight. "Bison-C" was a variant of Bison-B rebuilt as required for use as a maritime long-range reconnaissance platform for Soviet distant maritime forces. By virtue of its already extensive spectrum of assignments the nose section was enlarged to receive a larger radar installation than the B version.

The M-4 was an important military instrument of the Soviet Union for many years. It is thought that 93 of these machines were built, used later amongst other purposes as mid-air-refuellers. Production was terminated in 1963. According to NATO sources 75 M-4s were still in active service in the mid-1980s, the last of them were probably decommissioned towards the end of the 1990s.

The Bison-B was one of the first Soviet aircraft which could be refuelled in flight. (Schwede Archive)

A Bison-B escorted by a US Type F-14A Tomcat interceptor fighter. (Parson/USN)

Tupolev Tu-142

Towards the mid-1950s, at the suggestion of Admiral Arleigh Burke, the United States developed the strategic medium-range rocket UGM-27 which could be fired from so-called "Polaris" submarines. The first test on 20 July 1960 from aboard the USS George Washington caused such concern in the Soviet Union that the Government in Moscow saw the need to take corresponding counter-measures in order to restore the strategic balance. All design offices of the large Soviet aircraft manufacturers were called upon to submit plans for a maritime reconnaissance/ submarine-hunter to face the threat. To bring out a completely new design at this time would not only

have been costly but also extremely protracted, and so another solution was sought instead – for an aircraft already in existence. At once the search focussed on the long-range Tupolev bomber Tu-95 "Bear". The aircraft was extremely large and also had very long range, therefore it met all preconditions for operating over the sea, and using it as the basis, the Tupolev design team produced a maritime reconnaissance/anti-submarine warfare version by extending the fuselage by 1.7 metres to accommodate the comprehensive ELINT- and ECCM equipment. For storage of the sonobuoys used for submarine-detection a ventilated pressurized room

was devised. The weapons shafts, and release tubes for the buoys, are located aft. While the ILS- and radio aerials are below the fuselage, the direction-finding and satellite aerials are installed on top of it, and in the later version a MAD (Magnetic Anomaly Detector) was fitted at the tail. The almost new aircraft was given the designation Tu-142 and absolved its maiden flight on 18 June 1968 from Shukovski aerodrome south of Moscow with test pilot Vedernikov at the controls. Delivery to the operational units began in December 1972. Between 1968 and 1994 around 100 aircraft of this Type left the Tupolev assembly hangars.

In the course of time eight revised and modified variants of the Tu-142 emerged. The last series version of the Bear built was the Tu-142MR "Bear-J"

Aircraft Type:	Tupolev T-142
Purpose:	Maritime reconnaissance and submarine-hunter
Crew:	11-13 men
Engine:	4 x Kuznetzov NK-12MP turboprops (4 x 11,033 kW)
Wingspan:	50.00 m
Length:	53.08 m
Height:	12.12 m
Wing surface:	311.10 m²
Top speed:	925 km/hr
Cruising/patrol speed:	711 km/hr
Max. rate of climb:	n/a
Service ceiling:	12,000 m
Range:	6,500 km

operated as an airborne relay station for Russian submarines and also as a command post – a similar function to that of the US Boeing E-6 Mercury. Even today the MR is considered worldwide as the biggest platform for anti-submarine work. Tupolev also built numerous Tu-142MK-E as export versions, some of which are used operationally by India. In all probability India will keep its improved Tu-142 fleet operational until around 2020 before replacing it gradually with the much more modern Boeing P-1 Poseidon.

In the course of its history eight different redesigned variants of the Tu-124 emerged. (USN)

Also a classic amongst reconnaissance aircraft: The Tupolev TU-142M. (USN)

Between 1968 and 1994 around 100 Tupolev Tu-142M left the assembly lines. Here a TU-142M is seen in company with a US Navy Lockheed P-3 Orion. (USN)